Receiving the Vision

The
Anglican–Roman Catholic
Reality Today

A Study by the Third Standing Committee
of the
Episcopal Diocesan Ecumenical Officers
National Association of Diocesan Ecumenical Officers

David Bird
E. Rozanne Elder
R. William Franklin
Joan McGuire, O.P.
Dennis Mikulanis
Emmanuel Sullivan, S.A.

A Liturgical Press Book

THE LITURGICAL PRESS
Collegeville, Minnesota

Cover design by Greg Becker

1	2	3	4	5	6	7	8

Library of Congress Cataloging-in-Publication Data

Receiving the vision : the Anglican–Roman Catholic reality today : a study /
   by the Third Standing Committee of the Episcopal Diocesan Ecumenical
   Officers, National Association of Diocesan Ecumenical Officers:
   David Bird . . . [et al.].
     p.   cm.
   "A Liturgical Press book."
   Collaboration of six authors, three Anglican and three Roman Catholic,
presenting case studies on the interrelations in the United States of two
Christian communions—Foreword.
   Includes bibliographical references and index.
   ISBN 0-8146-2173-2
   1. Anglican Communion—Relations—Catholic Church. 2. Catholic
Church—Relations—Anglican Communion. 3. Interdenominational
cooperation. I. Bird, David. II. Third Standing Committee of the
Episcopal Diocesan Ecumenical Officers and the National Association
of Diocesan Ecumenical Officers.
BX5004.2.R43 1995
280'.042—dc20   94-35167
                                                    CIP

Contents

RECEPTION AND COMMUNITY

Abbreviations

AAS	*Acta Apostolica Sedis*
ARC	Anglican/Roman Catholic
ARCIC (I and II)	Anglican/Roman Catholic International Commission Commission I, 1969–1981; Commission II, 1982–
ARC/USA	Anglican/Roman Catholic Dialogue in the United States
BEM	*Baptism, Eucharist and Ministry;* The Lima Document of the World Council of Churches
CD	*Christus Dominus;* Vatican II Document on Ministry of Bishops
CDF	Congregation for the Doctrine of Faith
DV	*Dei Verbum;* Vatican II Document on Divine Revelation
ECUSA	Episcopal Church in the United States
EDEO	Episcopal Diocesan Ecumenical Officers
FR	*The Final Report* of ARCIC I
JES	*Journal of Ecumenical Studies*
LG	*Lumen Gentium;* Vatican II Dogmatic Constitution on the Church
NADEO	National Association of Diocesan Ecumenical Officers (Roman Catholic)
NCCB	National Conference of Catholic Bishops
UR	*Unitatis Redintegratio*; Vatican II Decree on Ecumenism
VENICE	*Authority in the Church: Elucidation,* ARCIC I, 1981
WCC	World Council of Churches

Foreword

This book represents a new and much needed genre of ecumenical literature. Its case studies provide an overview of the interrelations in the United States of two Christian communions that is both comprehensive and concrete and combines theological responsibility and popular accessibility. The case studies span the gamut from mixed marriages and local covenants to problems of dissent, heresy, episcopal authority, and women's ordination. They will open the eyes of neophytes, instruct the well-informed, and fascinate everyone. It is not only Anglicans and Roman Catholics who will be interested: those of other denominations will learn much about how to look at their own ecumenical situations. The more this book is a trend-setter, the better for the ecumenical movement.

The tone is realistic but not pessimistic. It becomes evident from the case studies that the ecumenical movement is inescapable. The intertwining of the churches proceeds apace no matter what the failed initiatives, disappointed hopes, and, in some areas, increasing difficulties. In one two-parish covenant, there was more enthusiasm on the Catholic than the Anglican side over the election of a woman to the Anglican episcopacy. It seems that Christians of diverse denominations cannot help affecting each other more and more whatever the ups or downs in official relations.

Moreover, as this volume illustrates, new successes in ecumenical endeavors are still possible. Here we have a ground-breaking collaborative effort of three Anglicans and three Roman Catholics which reads as a single whole, not a disparate collection. The fact that these authors are an official group, the Third EDEO/NADEO Standing Committee, adds to the authority of what they write without, fortunately, diminishing their candor.

This candor combined with ecumenical commitment is the crowning virtue of this work. When added to its other strengths, it makes this book as interesting and useful to those of us who are not Anglicans or Roman Catholics as to members of these two communions. It is tangible evidence of the deep, underlying unity of the church, and reminds us that our Lord's prayer that those who believe in him might be one (John 17:21) continues in our day to work mightily among us despite our divisions.

George Lindbeck
Pitkin Professor of Historical Theology
Yale University

Preface

Falling in love does not build a marriage. It is invariably a catalyst which draws two persons together. The relationship, however, is built upon mutual exploration, sharing, sacrifice, and long experience. An enduring marriage results from growth within each person and growth between persons, growth in relationship to the other person, and growth of the couple as a spiritual union.

Two Christian churches, like two persons, may rediscover each other after centuries of separation, and desire reunion. The enduring union they seek can only be forged by a long and not always easy process of growth. Each church must grow, and the relationship must grow, until a new level of mutual understanding has been reached.

After four hundred years of often acrimonious separation, Anglicans and Roman Catholics have slowly been rediscovering one another over the course of the past hundred years. Vatican Council II of the Roman Catholic Church marked a point of no return. The promulgation of its Decree on Ecumenism, *Unitatis Redintegratio,* which recognized, but did not define, the "special place" of Anglicanism, opened the way to the establishment of an official dialogue between the Roman Catholic Church and the Anglican communion. Positive relationships have existed since 1965 at the international level and between various national churches. The first Anglican-Roman Catholic International Commission (ARCIC) ended its work in 1981 with the publication of its *The Final Report,* a document containing agreed statements on Eucharistic doctrine, on ministry and ordination, and on authority in the church.[1] A second commission (ARCIC II) today continues its work and has issued agreed statements on salvation and the Church, the Church as communion, and moral teaching. Within the United States, a group representing the Episcopal Church and the National Conference of Catholic Bishops (ARC/USA) has been meeting, as

1. *The Final Report* (London: SPCK–Catholic Truth Society; Cincinnati: Forward Movement Publications, 1982). The Agreed Statements were published serially between 1972 and 1982 and are also available in Joseph W. Witmer and J. Robert Wright, eds., *Called to Full Unity: Documents on Anglican–Roman Catholic Relations 1966–1983* (Washington: United States Catholic Conference, 1986).

a rule, three times every two years since 1965. The foundation of these international and national dialogues does not signal a general Roman Catholic recognition of the ministry of the Anglican Churches. Yet these discussions are marked by the Roman Catholic recognition that Anglicanism occupies a special place among the separated communities of the West and by the clear vision which Anglicans and Roman Catholics share of the goal toward which we are pressing.

The bishops of Vatican II, recognizing that baptism incorporates Christians into one indivisible Body of Christ, spoke of our "real but imperfect communion." The communion or fellowship we share is often referred to by the Greek term *koinonia*. In *Church as Communion* the Anglican-Roman Catholic International Consultation members say of *koinonia*:

> The basic verbal form means "to share," "to participate," "to have part in," "to have something in common," or "to act together." The noun can signify fellowship or community. It usually signifies a relationship based on participation in a shared reality (e.g., 1 Cor 10:16).[2]

Our committee's vision is the rebuilding in all areas of the church's life of a loving, inclusive community rooted in our one baptism into Christ and the confession of the apostolic faith. Theological dialogue and local cooperation have furthered growth and mutual understanding, but they have not resolved all the difficulties hindering full and complete communion. By speaking and working together Anglicans and Roman Catholics have become aware that even difficulties which seem slight can sometimes present great obstacles that impede the growth of the relationship more than apparently serious theological problems. There has grown up among us a new honesty in recognizing and articulating differences in practice and discipline, and an understanding of how we have arrived at differing teachings. We have come to realize that discussion among theologians alone will not bring us to full and perfect communion. We need to understand and respect different ways of preserving and expressing the apostolic faith. We need to perceive within each other's tradition a common faith which alone can be the basis of union. This mutual process of discerning each other's traditions as a legitimate expression of Christian faith and practice is called "reception."

In our ecumenical context reception is the process whereby, under the guidance of the Holy Spirit, Anglicans and Roman Catholics at every level of their churches discern elements—in whole or in part—of the praxis, spirituality, and doctrine of the Church as authentic expressions of the Gospel and apostolic faith.

2. "Church as Communion," *Catholic International* 2:7 (April 1-14, 1981) 329.

In this modest study members of the Third EDEO/NADEO Standing Committee have attempted to highlight areas in which our two churches interact, and sometimes, with the best of intentions, misunderstand one another. By balancing specific case studies with theological reflection we hope to encourage Christians to deepen their relationship, not by covering over very real problems, but by setting them in context.

While ecumenical encounters between Anglicans and Roman Catholics, and any number of other churches, proceed at local, diocesan, national, and international levels, each church continues its own development, exercises its own discipline, and expounds its own doctrine. Some purely internal words and actions are perceived by members of the other church as good and proper, and are therefore well received. Others are perceived as threatening, slighting or irritating, and are not well received. Whatever the reception, the ecumenical relationship between the churches is affected. Some positions are received. Others are not received. Some local experiences raise theological questions and become ecumenical issues.

At the same time as theologians address and, to a heartening degree, resolve theological differences which have separated us for centuries, new very practical issues continue to arise. The dynamics of human relationships make this inevitable. A living relationship is ever open to change; only the dead are fossilized.

In assessing the progress we have made and the difficulties still before us, we have tried to keep people foremost in our mind. At the same time, our theological reflection places these issues in the broader context of our respective faith communities.

Three of the authors of this book are Roman Catholics, and three are Anglicans. And yet we can also be categorized in several other ways. Three of us are ordained, and three are lay. Two are women. Two are parish pastors. Two do ecumenical work professionally, and two teach at universities. Two belong to religious orders, and two have ties with monastic communities of the other church. Four studied in Europe, and two are working outside their homeland. This diversity over and beyond "denominational" lines has greatly enriched our work together.

Each chapter has been researched by one member of our committee and then discussed at length by the entire group. The conclusions therefore represent the consensus of the full committee.

Our committee is especially grateful to Sr. Joan McGuire, O.P., who has coordinated our efforts, and to Mrs. Barbara Feldt who has collated, typed and retyped, and uncomplainingly dealt with frequent revisions. These two persons have served well beyond the call of duty.

Our study encourages us despite the new climate of ecumenical debate created by the *Responses* of the Churches to the ARCIC *The Final Report* and now the ordination of women in the Church of England and other provinces. As we have discerned some of our disagreements we have been aware of the real communion which has allowed us to bring them to light. Differences of opinion have not necessarily followed ecclesiastical lines, a sign of the increasing plurality of both our churches. The more we have delved into the matters that divide us, the more we have recognized the extent to which we share a common faith and the more we have sensed that we are indeed part of one family under Christ.

RECEIVING
THE
VISION

1

Receiving the Vision

No Turning Back

Some words evoke strong feelings and excite the imagination. "Reception" is not that kind of word. Talk about "receiving" may mean any number of things. It is such an ordinary word that we can easily miss its deeper meaning. Reception can refer to the formal ceremony of acknowledging an important event or person. It can refer to an attitude in a personal encounter, as when we speak of a warm or cool reception. It can even describe the functioning of our radio or television. "To receive" often means the simple acceptance of something, as when we receive a gift, a payment due, or an apology. Still, "reception" has a deeper meaning. It can refer to the capability of holding or containing something in such a way that what is received becomes part of the whole—the container and what is contained, integrated, made one thing. For example, in jurisprudence "reception" refers to a process whereby the developing nations of present-day Western Europe took the older legal system of the Roman Empire into their new structures of government. We ought not, then, to let the more ordinary meanings of "reception" cause us to underestimate its value in history. Moreover it has a deep theological significance when we come to speak of the unity of the church through the ages. In the present life of churches seeking to renew, rediscover, and reintegrate a visible and credible measure of Christian unity, the word has taken on new ecumenical significance.

Reception: A Spiritual Process

Reception, as we use the term, is first and foremost a spiritual process. As a process, reception begins with the recognition that the Church is a communion of communions, however imperfect or impaired its present state of communion may be. This communion is rooted in the very nature of the Triune God in whose life the church shares in its union with

Christ.[1] Further, this spiritual reality may be traced to the activity of the Holy Spirit in the life of the church. An openness to the active presence of God's Spirit in our still separated churches is indispensable if we are to receive the Christian tradition anew and live in the spirit of the original apostolic community.[2] This relation to the apostolic tradition is not a matter of ecclesiastical ideology or polity. It signifies a historical continuity with the reality of the Lord Jesus and those first disciples, which enables us to be faithful to the purpose and mission of the church in its prophetic calling to be a community living in and for God's world. The Holy Spirit ensures such continuity and fidelity. This is our common understanding of the apostolic tradition. An eminent theologian describes the notion of reception as "an openness to the apostolic tradition."[3] This openness necessarily and logically implies the reception of the ecumenical movement into the life of our churches. The ecumenical movement is nothing less than a movement of the Holy Spirit which enables us to receive the apostolic tradition anew.[4]

Reception is essential in the life of the church in both its teaching and its spiritual life. Reception takes place under the guidance of the Spirit as faith is actually lived out by Christians. The Holy Spirit enables our separated churches to welcome new and fresh expressions of faith in the rediscovery of our common faith. The Spirit brings the gift of discernment to the ecumenical dialogue by which we begin to recognize what is in continuity with apostolic faith. Thus older ecumenical problems, such as the "filioque" in the Nicene Creed, are seen to be capable of resolution. The use of the vernacular in the liturgy makes it far easier to see a real convergence in the worship of various church traditions. Scholarship within the biblical tradition is making the Scriptures a powerful and preeminent binding force in experiencing our common faith. The ecumenical movement itself gives new meaning to our basic and essential oneness in Christ. The Spirit working within our limitations enables the churches to harmonize renewed insights in the mutual exchange of formal theological dialogue and in the everyday experience of church life. In its response to the Lima Document, *Baptism, Eucharist and Ministry,*[5] the former Lu-

---

1. See Emmanuel Sullivan, "Koinonia As a Meta-Model for Future Church Unity," *Ecumenical Trends* 18:1 (January 1989) 1–7, with Lutheran and Anglican responses following.

2. See John Zizioulas, "The Theological Problem of 'Reception,' " *One in Christ* 21 (1985) 187–193.

3. Myroslaw Tataryn, "Karl Rahner and the Nature of Reception," *One in Christ* 25 (1989) 76.

4. See *Unitatis Redintegratio*, nn. 1,4; *Dei Verbum*, n. 8; *Lumen Gentium*, n. 15. All approved by Vatican Council II.

5. *Baptism, Eucharist and Ministry,* Faith and Order Paper III, World Council of Churces, Geneva (1982).

theran Church in America noted that "reception ultimately will not be a matter of documents but a renewed people under the Spirit expressing their unity in Christ."[6]

Reception is often thought of as a willingness on the part of churches to receive the results of ecumenical dialogue as an expression, wholly or in part, of the faith of particular churches. It goes further than that, however. It is the willingness of one church to receive from another church a practice or tradition which it finds consistent with its own ecclesial life. Thus already churches such as those of the Anglican and Roman Catholic communions experience a stage of unity which is a kind of covenantal relationship committed to finding a more perfect stage of church unity. The commitment is to find that fullness of unity willed by our Lord for the church by the means the Holy Spirit provides.

This vision of Christian unity and the genuine desire for it draws on the prayer of Jesus recorded in John 17:

> I do not pray for these only, but also for those who believe in me through their word, that they may all be one, even as thou, Father, art in me and I in thee, that they also may be one in us, so that the world may believe that thou hast sent me (John 17:20).

This prayer might be considered a first principle of the ecumenical movement, and is certainly central to it. Even churches conditioned and restricted by a particular ecclesiology can commit their members to praying and working for the unity Christ wills by the means he chooses.[7]

The commitment to ecumenism varies with the churches involved in the movement. For some churches, Christian unity is taken to be a very loose association of churches. For others, it is a kind of federation of churches that allows a high degree of autonomy and diversity. For still others, it is more centralized in authority and structure. Thus theologies of ecumenism differ, but whatever understanding of the church underpins these theologies, ecumenism demands some definite commitment to move beyond a utopian vision and a vague eschatological hope existing apart from the real commitment which might lead to the realization here and now of the church's witness and mission. Prayer for unity will al-

---

6. "The Response of LCA to *BEM, Faith and Order Paper 111*," adopted by the 1984 Convention of the Lutheran Church of America. This Church is now fully integrated with the Evangelical Church in America (ELCA) as of 1988.

7. Such was the case of the Roman Catholic Church until Vatican Council II, when a genuine development of its doctrine vis-a-vis other separated Christian Churches and ecclesial communities took place. Such a development, however, is rooted in the older theology of the Church as a communion of communions. Roman Catholic theology is conditioned in this matter by its understanding that the unity Christ wills for the church "subsists in" the Roman Church. This is expressed in *Unitatis Redintegratio*, n.3, and *Lumen Gentium*, n.8.

ways remain the mainspring of ecumenical activity, but always with the understanding that we must work for what we pray. In appropriating the prayer of Jesus we enflesh it with our commitment to refine our understanding and commitment to Christian unity.[8] Hence our churches stand in need of vision, prophetic activity, and a spirit of reception to ensure honest-to-God ecumenism.

In their mutual commitment to ecumenism, Anglicans and Roman Catholics think of a fullness of unity and communion, organic and visible, which nonetheless is a workable diversity based upon inherited traditions of discipline, liturgy, and devotion. This unity of diversity is an authentic expression of our mutual understanding of the church as a communion of communions.

The spirit of receptivity has to be developed and synchronized with the overall growth of the ecumenical movement. This requires due regard for how theologians and church leaders deal with ecumenism. Their function is to monitor attentively and respectfully the actual experiences of Christians in other churches. The reception process takes into account decisions taken by particular churches which may affect the ecumenical movement. The members of a particular church need to discern that their decisions are faithful to the New Testament and in the Spirit of Christ. As Lukas Vischer says: "For such a reception to take place, churches are called to develop a 'spirituality of reception,' a readiness for reforms and structures of common decision making. Every consensus invites the churches to express jointly the single tradition in their midst and newly make it their own."[9]

Formation

Ecumenism is a process of formation in church members. Formation is closely related to reception. The lay and clerical members of our churches stand in need of spiritual preparation in order to enter into the spirit of ecumenism and to receive the fruits of the movement into the life of their churches. Formation is not to be equated with information. Of course Christians in all churches need some basic information concerning the doctrine and practice of other churches. Formation also demands that we have a basic grasp of the general principles governing the ecumenical movement. We will return to these in the last chapter. Formation also means that we have to try and understand the different approaches and prin-

8. See Emmanuel Sullivan, *Prayer for Unity,* a publication of the Graymoor Ecumenical Institute (1988), available from Graymoor, Garrison, N.Y. 10524.

9. Lukas Vischer, "The Process of 'Reception' in the Ecumenical Movement," *Midstream,* 23 (1984) 221–233.

ciples proper to different churches as they seek to share in the search for Christian unity through the ecumenical movement.

Whatever our starting point in the ecumenical venture, our churches must consciously will to move beyond the limits imposed on them at the present time. Ecumenism is a convergence process, leading to full visible unity and flowering in authentic diversity, yet lending the utmost credibility to the church's mandate to proclaim a gospel of reconciliation for all. Thus understood ecumenism is a renewed search for ways to express catholicity as a mark of the Christian church.

Ecumenical formation involves three stages of development. First, churches come to recognize other churches as Christian communities of faith. This means a recognition of such communities in their ecclesial status and not simply as a community of well intentioned individuals. This, for example, was the basis at the time of the Vatican Council II for the Roman Catholic reformulation of its theology. Other churches were to be understood as churches of the Anglican communion and as churches of the Reformation. With this new understanding the Roman Catholic Church could enter the ecumenical movement on an equal footing with other churches of the movement. On this basis it is now possible for both Roman Catholics and Anglicans to state together that they are seeking full communion.

The second stage of ecumenical formation consists in learning to read ecumenical texts. Thus, when we read such texts as *The Final Report* of ARCIC I, the Lima Document, and the Lutheran–Roman Catholic Statement on Justification, we must do so in a spirit of openness and according to the methodology adopted by those who wrote them, and not according to a set of theological principles developed and pre-established within our own denominational frame of reference. The basic question to be asked in reading such texts is: to what extent is your church able to recognize in this text the faith of the church throughout the ages?

The third stage in ecumenical formation follows from the openness consequent on reading such texts. In this stage we find our theological thinking, our spiritual understanding, and our attitudes and outlook on other churches transformed by a sense of a fundamental communion with other Christians in the communion of the church, impaired and imperfect as it presently is. This, in turn, nourishes a real desire for full Christian unity, and the desire forms an ecumenical spirituality which is the very soul of ecumenism. "Therefore, receive one another just as Christ has received you to the glory of God" (Rom 15:7). John Zizioulas reminds us that "reception is not a matter of texts alone, but of churches and people. In the very act of reacting to texts the churches enter a process of receiving each other as Churches."[10] Thus the second stage in ecumen-

10. Zizioulas, 193.

ical formation leads into this third stage as the members of our churches move from a new respect for the faith that is in other Christians to a new will and desire for Christian unity.

The Sensus Fidelium

This will and desire for Christian unity introduces a further notion which we express in its Latin form. *Sensus fidelium* is the special term used to express and describe that instinct for the true faith found in all faithful members of our churches. It is a feeling or instinct for what faith actually entails for the life and mission of the church, and is the activity of the Holy Spirit in the hearts of believers. God's people do not accept merely human words but truly the very word of God.[11] As such the *sensus fidelium* is essential to understanding the process of reception in ecumenical formation.

"Reception is not a dry practical idea."[12] Behind the word "reception" lies a spiritual concept and an essential element of Christian theology that takes into account the grace of the Holy Spirit. In its ecumenical context this requires the churches to examine their fidelity to the apostolic tradition. Churches ought to feel free enough at this stage of the ecumenical movement to challenge one another to do the same.[13] The willingness to challenge one another as we walk the ecumenical pilgrim way gives further assurance that our discernment in the Spirit is real. Moreover, such challenges reveal a new and larger context for the truth we seek behind our various doctrinal formulations. This ought not to damage ecumenical relations because it must be done in a spirit inspired by a genuine desire for unity.

This desire for unity is itself a mark of what we have called the *sensus fidelium*, a feeling for the demands of the apostolic faith and fidelity to the tradition therein, a fidelity to the mind of Christ for his church. It is all part of the church's prophetic impulse to live, pray, and work together even now in our separated condition. We are the Body of Christ, and our desire for unity is a recognition and reception of what the Holy Spirit has been doing in our churches during the long years of schism and separation. It is neither naive optimism nor wishful thinking to suppose that during these long periods our churches have developed particular gifts of the Spirit to enliven the church in its life and mission. Their very diversity in style and practices enhances the catholicity of the church lest we

11. See 1 Thessalonians 2:13.

12 Zizioulas, 190.

13. See J. M. R. Tillard, "Reception: A Time to Beware of False Steps," *Ecumenical Trends* 14:10 (November 1985) 145–148.

confuse uniformity with unity. The ecumenical movement has led to a new respect for pluralism in expressing our unity in faith. A new sense of catholicity is evolving in the churches of the ecumenical movement. "Pluriformity is not an unfortunate concession to human weakness, nor is the Christian revelation receivable and expressible in one way only."[14]

Denominations cannot be renewed in isolation from one another. Something more than internal reform is needed. Renewal in isolation, as we know well from our sixteenth-century experience, becomes a counter-reformation which only serves to reinforce the walls of separation. Jean Tillard says that even if such renewal and reformation led to a deeper personal holiness, it would not be faithful to the Gospel because as a true community of faith we are not what we are supposed to be. Referring to the separated churches, he says that "even if some of them are convinced they possess everything that is required to be truly the Church of God" they are marked by failure, for the Church's mission "does not consist in an addition of faithfulness but in a common faithfulness."[15]

Local Ecumenism

Essential to the reception process and to the development of the *sensus fidelium* is the bringing of ever-increasing numbers of the laity and clergy in our churches into a formal commitment to work as loyal members of their respective churches for the unity of the church. It is at this local level of church life that Christians have a very practical experience of the need and urgency of Christian unity. If local ecumenism is to make its indispensable contribution to the reception of the ecumenical movement, it must get into the bloodstream of the local church and become a dimension of church activity and planning. All too often ecumenism is perceived as optional or a concession to the enthusiasm of a particular group within the parish or congregation, and thus ecumenical witness is trivialized and diminished in the public forum. Even now, in our state of imperfect communion as churches, the commitment to be faithful to Christ in seeking reconciliation and unity among churches is a powerful witness, and serves to reduce the danger of scandal associated with a divided Christendom. This witness to the world cannot be effective unless there is greater involvement on the part of local churches. Local churches need some experience of unity, an experience involving a notable number of the faithful

14. Robert Butterworth, "Reception and Pluriformity," *The Month* 18:10 (1985) 348–358. This article is an important resource for our study of reception since it was written in the context of *The Final Report* of ARCIC I.

15. Tillard, "The Call for a Judgement upon the Churches and the Ecumenical Movement," *Midstream* 23 (1984) 234–250.

in all our churches. The local church is the test for the reception of the ecumenical movement. Dispersed individuals or isolated authorities cannot do it. Everything that is part of church structure—discipline and liturgy, preaching and teaching, a sense of mission, the life of devotion and pious practice—all must be connected to a sincere will for Christian unity.

It is at this point in the reception process that the work of pastoral leadership is very important. First, the vision presented in the prayer of our Lord in John 17 has to be communicated to the local congregation. Second, the local church must gain a sense of value of the life and mission it is called upon to manifest by its presence in the civil life of the wider community. Within the parish or congregation the quality of preaching and teaching is paramount. Clerical and lay, preachers and teachers, must strive to bring church members to an ecumenical way of being Christian.

Ecumenism always entails a measure of conversion. Here by "conversion" we mean an ecumenical experience of faith. In a report issued by a study group set up by the Faith and Order Commission of the National Council of Churches (usa),[16] a number of "ecumenical findings" were published. The very first set of "findings" deals with conversion:

> Finding 1.   A Christian's commitment to ecumenism seems to begin with a "holy discontent" over the division and diversities among Christians.
>
> Finding 2.   Because "ecumenical conversion," like every real conversion, is always a work of the Holy Spirit, its precise course cannot be determined in advance.
>
> Finding 3.   Ecumenical "conversion" is, at least in part, the process whereby God changes us through our dialogue partners.

Most Christians are aware of the importance of conversion in ordinary Christian life but are likely to overlook or even reject the need for it as a spiritual reality in their church's search for Christian unity. Individual conversion is recognized by a change in a person's behavior; it is not generally thought of in relation to the witness of the church as a community of faith with a message of reconciliation for the wider civic community. Reception of its very nature implies conversion. If the conversion is the real thing, it will show itself in conversation and dialogue, in cooperative ventures of a social nature, in a willingness to learn and receive from others and to be changed in our very consciousness. Such a conversion

16. *Ecumenical Findings: Toward a Conciliar Fellowship.* This is a report on the bilateral and multilateral dialogues from a study of the Commission on Faith and Order of the National Council of Churches (usa) from 1982–1987, available from the Commission's Office, Room 872, 475 Riverside Drive, New York, N.Y. 10115-1500.

or reception deepens our basic commitment to Christ and refines our appreciation of one another's ecclesiastical traditions. Conversion, with its spirit of openness, does not demand that we sacrifice either our conscientious convictions or our search for the truth. Rather, the whole atmosphere of our churches is charged with respect and affection, by which all are brought to repentance.[17]

Conclusion

We have been reflecting on the spiritual nature of reception. Reception's source is the central place of the Holy Spirit in Christian life. Ecumenical receptivity is envisioned in the prayer of Jesus "that all may be one . . . that the world may believe." We appropriate this prayer and relate it to the Christian vocation of giving prophetic witness to the reconciling love of God in Christ for all people. This becomes real and particular to the extent that it becomes local, and this happens through dialogue, general association, and interaction among Christians across denominational lines. In this way the churches are brought to mature Christian formation through a kind of conversion. This creates a new sense of faithfulness to Christ and a richer *sensus fidelium*, and this makes the life and mission of Jesus the life and mission of the church.

In the following chapters we will be looking at the reception of the teachings and disciplines of our two churches. Even in separation, we discover, Anglicans and Roman Catholics are so close that events in one faith community affect members of the other and elicit a response. Whether critical or approving, this spontaneous response, from bishops, clergy, and laity, constitutes a form of reception (or, as we have sometimes called it here, non-reception). Some things are received by both communities; some find reception officially only in one but generate discussion in the other; some are emphatically not received. Among Christians today there are many shades of opinion and reception is not easily determined or evaluated. General tendencies can, however, be observed and it is to these that we now turn.

17. *Ibid.*, 4–7.

LAITY
AND
COMMUNITY

2

The People of God

Prophets and Pilgrims

Laypersons in past generations were apt to identify strongly with their own church tradition, and speak—and think—disparagingly of other faith communities. As small communities have broken down in America, and the church has generally lost its role as the chief expression of ethnic and community identity, has this post-reformation exclusivity changed for the average lay Christian?

We can regard the churches historically, institutionally, or theologically and find greatly differing forms of polity and worship. We can view them sociologically and discern (according to James Hopewell in his recent *Congregation*[1]) that doctrine often has very little to do with membership and that local myth frequently outweighs received tradition. We can study them juridically, as inexorably all inter-church dialogues are drawn to do, and posit theoretical and practical claims to authority. We can also, with less scholarly apparatus, regard them experientially, and this is, in fact, how the vast majority of Christians, the so-called average man and woman in the pew, thinks of them.

While many laypersons might declare that their own faith community most fully expresses the Christian faith, few are prepared to articulate theological dissimilarity. If called to identify areas of difference, they tend to remark on varying exegetical or liturgical customs rather than on theological doctrine. As Hopewell says, "In a local church, members participate in religion more readily than they explain it."[2] Furthermore, except for those in ethnic enclaves, the laity, however strong their loyalty to their own church, are very often drawn by ties of family, friendship, and profession to meet regularly with members of other faith communities. Most American extended families include members of several churches. Metho-

---

1. James F. Hopewell, *Congregation: Stories and Structure* (Philadelphia: Fortress Press, 1987).
2. *Ibid.,* 68.

dist parents may have adult children active in Roman Catholic, Quaker, and Evangelical churches. Each belongs to what the seventeenth-century Anglican, Lancelot Andrewes,[3] and the twentieth-century Roman Catholic, Yves Congar,[4] called "particular churches," with particular disciplines, particular doctrinal formulations, and particular ways of worship.

Our two particular churches, the Anglican and Roman Catholic, are in real but incomplete communion. There are, however, particular churches in full communion with each other within both the Roman Catholic and the Anglican traditions. For a particular church to be in full communion with the Roman Catholic Church means that the Roman Catholic Church receives as proper to the particular church its liturgical, spiritual, disciplinary, and theological traditions. Full communion exists between the Melkite Church, which follows the Eastern Rite, and the Roman Catholic Church, which follows the Western Rite. The Anglican Communion at the Chicago-Lambeth Quadrilateral of 1888 stated:

> That in the opinion of this Conference, the following Articles supply a basis on which approval may be by God's blessing towards Home Reunion: a) The Holy Scriptures of the Old and New Testaments as "containing all things necessary to salvation," and as being the rule and ultimate standard of faith. b) The Apostles' Creed, as the Baptismal Symbol; and the Nicene Creed, as the sufficient statement of the Christian faith. c) The two Sacraments ordained by Christ Himself—Baptism and the Supper of the Lord—ministered with unfailing use of Christ's words of Institution, and of the elements ordained by Him. d) The Historic Episcopate, locally adapted in the methods of its administration to the varying needs of the nations and peoples called of God into the Unity of His Church.[5]

Full communion exists between the Anglican communion and the Old Catholic Church in Europe in union with the See of Utrecht.

3. Every one of which "hath power to begin a custom, and that custom power to bind her own children to it, provided her private custom affront not the general, received by others. . . ." Sermon for Easter (April 5, 1618) in *Ninety-six Sermons by the Right Honourable and Reverend Father in God Lancelot Andrewes. . .*, II (Oxford: J. H. Parker, 1841, New York, 1967) 412.

4. See *I Believe in the Holy Spirit, 2: The Lord and Giver of Life* (Collins-Seabury, 1983) 26. Congar adopted this term to distinguish the local churches (which he identifies with the dioceses—see the document of Vatican II, *Lumen Gentium,* 23: 1 and 26) from "the Church which presents a particular aspect" in language, recruitment, and historical uniqueness.

5. *The Book of Common Prayer and Administration of the Sacraments and Other Rites and Ceremonies of the Church* (New York: The Church Hymnal Corporation, 1979) 877-878.

Some would staunchly declare their conviction that the church extends beyond their own church body, and some would not. Yet in churches in the United States today, few would stoutly refuse to recognize members of churches not their own as Christians, or consign them, as did many of their forebears, on that account to hell.

Anglican–Roman Catholic Dialogue

Dialogue between Roman Catholics and Anglicans (Episcopalians) has been officially in progress since 1965 in the United States (ARC/USA) and since 1969 at the international level (ARCIC). In these years agreed statements have been issued, though not all yet officially received, on the Eucharist, on ministry, on authority in the church, on salvation, on community, and on moral discipline. In many places Roman Catholic and Episcopal bishops find it increasingly to their advantage to cooperate on some social issues and to join in non-Eucharistic worship. How much these evidences of fellowship affect the average "person in the pew" is, however, open to question. The parish continues to be the focus of Christian community for most Roman Catholics and Episcopalians, and although at the parochial level contact between the two traditions has moved from latent suspicion and competitive regard to an implicit realization that the other is an historically and theologically conditioned expression of a shared faith, how much real contact exists between the two faith communities at the local level is uncertain.

Members of many churches across the country work together to fight social injustice and to relieve suffering, and each may think of this activity as an imperative of Christ's call to visit the sick and imprisoned in his name. But they seldom consciously think of their work together as an ecumenical activity. At the same time, the formation and growth of a layperson's faith is seldom coterminous with his or her parish or diocese. In an age of almost universal literacy, laypersons hungry for spiritual nourishment take it where they find it, and while their parish experience may lead them to choose "spiritual reading" from traditions sympathetic to their own, book sales indicate a strongly ecumenical eclecticism. Retreats and workshops frequently draw persons from various, quite disparate, churches. Ties of family and friendship lead people to visit churches outside their own tradition for special occasions or for occasional Sunday worship. Marriage not infrequently causes one person to leave his or her tradition for the partner's church, or it causes two persons to leave their original faith communities to settle on a "compromise" third. In all these crossings-over new customs may startle or please and differing discipline may delight or annoy. The Eucharist, sacrament of unity, causes the greatest obstacle to uniting in worship. Many visitors to a tradition other than their own find injunctions against Eucharistic sharing incomprehensible. Some experience anguish over separation; some accept the situation with indifference; some simply ignore the rules imposed by the clerical guardians of the tradition.

Within the profound depth of our real communion and the limits of our incomplete communion, Anglican Roman-Catholic families, shared parishes and cooperating dioceses demonstrate in a very particular and public way the existence of communion within the church. We present in the next chapter stories of enrichment as well as of pain experienced by ARC families. In the following chapter we look at the successes and disappointments of ARC parishes and dioceses as they struggle to work and worship together in Christ's name so that the world may believe.

3

Anglican–Roman Catholic Families

Signs of Unity Bearing the Weight of Disunity

ARCIC I in *The Final Report* states, "Union with God in Christ Jesus through the Spirit is the heart of Christian *koinonia.*" The report continues, "communion with one another is entailed by our communion with God in Christ."[1] *Koinonia* or communion is a base and a goal of the Anglican Church and the Roman Catholic Church. Communion is perhaps most visibly realized by Anglican–Roman Catholic (ARC) families. It may be that those who live their daily lives as an ARC family are the most authentic ecumenical prophets and pilgrims within our two churches. ARC families demonstrate in a very particular and public way "receiving communities" within the church, especially when the reception of their marriage covenant includes reception of the extended family and the church of the other. Two theological concepts seem to be intensifying the prophetic witness of ARC families: linking ecumenical families to church unity, and defining the family as a domestic church. We consider anew these concepts. We then hear the stories of six domestic ARC churches. These families witness to the promise of unity while their pilgrimages reveal the pain of disunity.

Ecumenical Families and Christian Unity

The pilgrim feet of Episcopal and Roman Catholic brides and grooms have moved from Roman Catholic sacristies to Catholic or Episcopal churches for the celebration of sacramental union in marriage. The Roman Catholic Church, seemingly the more reluctant partner, has also had pilgrim feet. Fr. George Kilcourse in his *Ecumenical Marriages* traces the official church attitude on the ecumenical significance of ecumenical marriages. He notes that although Pope Paul VI's 1970 apostolic letter

1. *The Final Report,* "Introduction," n. 5.

Matrimonia Mixta states that mixed marriages "do not, except in some cases, help in reestablishing unity among Christians," John Paul II in 1992 addressed ecumenical families in England as you who "live in your marriage the hopes and difficulties of the path to Christian unity."[2] Fr. John Hotchkin finds links between family and church reconciliation in the exhortation *Familiaris Consortio* by the present bishop of Rome on the Catholic family. Father Hotchkin states:

> No doubt for the first time in an official document of this character, "Familiaris Consortio" links the sacramental life of the family to the ecumenical quest for Christian unity in a direct and positive way. Having said that every family is called by God to the joyous experience of reconciliation, communion reestablished and unity restored, the apostolic exhortation continues: "In particular, participation in the sacrament of reconciliation and in the banquet of the one body of Christ offers to the Christian family the grace and responsibility of overcoming every division and of moving toward the fullness of communion willed by God responding in this way to the ardent desire of the Lord 'that they may be one' " ("Familiaris Consortio" n. 21). This teaching, it would seem, has a special applicability to many mixed marriage households and will be seen by them as offering much more guidance in their situation than the more general maxim that sacramental sharing is not to be used "indiscriminately" as a means of furthering Christian unity.[3]

Father Hotchkin explains that this new context sets no new norms. *Familiaris Consortio* states that the norms used now by the Pontifical Council for Promoting Christian Unity are to be followed.[4]

The Anglican and Roman Catholic bishops of Illinois also relate ecumenical families to the quest for Christian unity in their document on Anglican-Roman Catholic marriages, *A Unique Grace*. The bishops state that the sacramental way of life of ARC families "already binds them into a unity that their church communions still need to bring to perfection."[5] The bishops further emphasize the ecumenical effort of ARC families by stating that "their marriage vows effect that unity for which their separated Churches long."[6] The bishops continue:

2. George Kilcourse, *Ecumenical Marriage: An Orientation Booklet for Engaged Couples, Families, Pastoral Ministers, Religious Educators* (National Association of Diocesan Ecumenical Officers, 1987) 5.

3. John Hotchkin, " 'Familiaris Consortio': New Light on Mixed Marriages," *One in Christ* (1986) 77, 78.

4. *Ibid.*, 79.

5. Bishops of Illinois, *A Unique Grace:* A Statement on the Marriage between Episcopal and Roman Catholic Christians in Illinois (Chicago: Catholic Conference of Illinois, 1990) 7.

6. *Ibid.*, 6.

The eschatological dimension of Episcopal and Roman Catholic marriages gives the separated churches hope that the future holds the restoration of the One Undivided Church of Christ; for its unity is already among us enfleshed in the union of Episcopal and Roman Catholic couples.[7]

When we realize that the unity of the one undivided Church of Christ is enfleshed in the union of Episcopal and Roman Catholic couples, we can state that each partner "receives" the church of the other.

There are further implications. An ARC union provides each spouse with reception not only into the church but also into the family of the other. Both the hyphenated family names of modern usage, and the long standing canonical understanding (Roman Catholic Code, Canon 109) of the relationship of two families joined by the marriage of members, reflect the reception by each spouse of the family of the partner. Ideally, within an ARC marriage the spouses receive and make their own not only an Anglican or Roman Catholic partner but also an Anglican or Roman Catholic extended family and an Anglican or Roman Catholic Church. Admitting then that to at least a minimal degree an ARC marriage brings into the union the Roman Catholic and Anglican Churches of the two spouses, the ecumenical importance of ARC marriages is evident.

Family as Domestic Church

Vatican Council II in its church-as-a-communion ecclesiology and its theology of the laity deems the family a "domestic church" where parents minister to their children. The sacred place of "family is, so to speak, the domestic church" in which "the parents are, by their word and example, the first preachers of the faith to their children."[8] John Paul II has developed the idea of domestic church: "in the case of baptized people, the family, called together by word and sacrament as the church of the home, is both teacher and mother, the same as the world wide Church."[9] An Anglican–Roman Catholic family, therefore, constitutes an ARC domestic church, a church that is both Anglican and Roman Catholic, a church that exists within churches which are not in visible unity. An ARC domestic church is one church even as the family members continue to belong to two churches that are united really but imperfectly.

7. *Ibid.,* 7.
8. *Lumen Gentium,* n. 11.
9. *Familaris Consortio,* Apostolic Exhortation on the Catholic Family (Chicago: Archdiocese of Chicago) November 22, 1981, 38.

Six Domestic ARC Churches

In another joint Episcopal–Roman Catholic statement on marriage guidelines the bishops of Louisiana state that "in an Episcopal–Roman Catholic marriage both churches hold the sacramental nature of marriage in even higher esteem than their difference in traditions and discipline."[10]

That the sacramental nature of their marriage is held in higher esteem than their differences in traditions and discipline becomes apparent in the stories told of life in their domestic churches by six ARC spouses. Their six stories[11] reveal the hope and the weight of the restoration of the one undivided Church of Christ borne by ARC domestic churches.

Domestic ARC Church A. A twenty-nine-year-old Episcopalian and her forty-year-old Roman Catholic husband, both of whom have had no religious education in their churches, have a two-year-old child baptized in the Roman Catholic Church. Their story:

> We now have a two-year-old and another on the way. Before we could marry in the Catholic Church I had to sign forms saying I'd raise my children as Catholics. I refused at first, but was told we couldn't be married otherwise.
>
> Knowing my husband's strict upbringing in his church, I agreed (not willingly). We have since had our daughter baptized Catholic, as our next child will be also. I feel a little forced, and some resentment about it. We all go to the Catholic Church every Sunday and holidays. We all go to my Episcopal Church at least every other Sun-

---

10. Episcopalian and Roman Catholic Bishops of Louisiana, "Louisiana Guidelines for Episcopal–Roman Catholic Marriages," *Origins* 13:45 (April 19, 1984) 746.

11. Space required us to limit the number of stories reported in this publication. For ongoing information on ecumenical marriages see *The Ark,* a Publication of the American Association of Interchurch Families, c/o Highlands Community Ministries, Louisville, Ky 40204.

Questionnaires were distributed to all EDEO/NADEO directors. Thirty-seven questionnaires were returned from ARC spouses ranging from twenty-six to seventy-nine years of age. Spouses responded from Virginia, Michigan, Arizona, Arkansas, California, Connecticut, Oklahoma, Kansas, and Wisconsin. Three were unmarked. Communication was also received from diocesan leadership in Kansas City (Kansas), Dubuque, Orange, Albuquerque, Green Bay, Albany, San Francisco, Little Rock, and Oklahoma City, and from parish leadership in Virginia and Kansas.

The authors express their appreciation to ARC spouses who made this report possible, both those who requested that their names not be used in publication, and the following: Leonard and Tina Darling, Phil and Val Porter, Mr. and Mrs. William H. Morrow, Nancy M. and Raymond S. Hall, Sr., Robert and Linda Bushor, Helen Dwyer Lundquist, Thomas and Ann Troy, Lee and Bonnie Startt, Scott and Patrice Tompkins, Mr. and Mrs. Michael J. Bousquet, Mr. and Mrs. Robert Kentner, Ernest B. and Bernedette Ingle Pflug, Ann and Clint Turner, Mr. and Mrs. James Leich, Jr.,

day. We both participate in both services (Communion, etc.). My husband has agreed to allow the children to go to Sunday school in the Episcopal Church if they want (when the time comes) along with the weekly CCD. He attends my church, but says he can't help with any of the service (serving, etc.). He receives Communion at my church, but says it doesn't mean anything to him. I also participate in his church (Communion etc.), but don't quite feel at home. We agree that neither of us want to change our religion, and so we have to accept the things we don't like about the other's services. Our daughter seems quite adjusted to both churches and asks to see the other priest when we're at one church. The services are so close in structure it gets boring at times. Sometimes even the same songs are sung. When our children turn eighteen they can decide for themselves which church to keep, or both.

His family has accepted me as Episcopalian and I feel they think more of me now since I haven't let them pressure me into changing churches like the other daughters-in-law. We talk freely about both churches. I don't know what they think about having the children exposed to the Episcopal Church. The Catholic and Episcopal Churches are so close in their values and services that it's not difficult to go to both churches. It would be very hard for other denominations to fit in though.

Domestic ARC Church B. A Roman Catholic wife and her husband who is an Episcopalian have five children who were baptized and attend religion education in the Roman Catholic Church. The whole family worships regularly in a Roman Catholic Church in the winter. In the summer the husband worships in an Episcopal Church. His religious education was in another Christian church. Their story:

> We were raised in traditional Catholic and Protestant ways, but when we began dating during our college years (early 70s), we had both lapsed from religious practices.
>
> I believe it was the grace of the sacrament of matrimony that brought me back into the fold. I went to confession and after the wedding began attending weekly Mass.
>
> Our wedding was in a Catholic church performed by a Catholic priest with my husband's uncle, an Episcopal priest, assisting.

Marilyn Magdefran Kirby, William and Pamela Jones, Ed and Pauline Porter, Mike and Annette Cherua, and George F. Little.

We also express appreciation to diocesan and parish leadership who responded: Rev. George Kilcourse, Rev. Phil Hoffmann, Rev. Msgr. Lawrence Baird, Rev. Ernest R. Falardeau, S.S.S., Rev. Robert L. Ferring, Rev. Charles Fisher, Msgr. Henry Gardner, Rowland M. Sinnamon, Rev. John J. Keane, S.A., Rev. Elmer A. Klenke, Rev. Joe Lehman, Sr. Catherine Markey, Rev. John P. Ryan, Rev. Raymond Barton, and those who submitted the questionnaire to ARC couples.

We really get along quite well because my husband believes in the real presence of Jesus in the Eucharist and has permission to receive him at Mass. We spend our summers on a resort island where his Episcopal roots are strong, and so he attends the Episcopal church there.

Our biggest hurdle is the birth control issue. We have five children, and my husband sees no harm in beginning contraceptive practices while I strongly disagree. We've put our trust in the Lord to get us through this too. (Remember us in your prayers.)

Domestic ARC Church C. A thirty-eight-year-old wife who is a Roman Catholic and a forty-one-year-old husband who is an Episcopalian were married in 1975. They have a nine-year-old child baptized in the Roman Catholic Church. The wife and child worship regularly in the Roman Catholic Church. The husband does not worship regularly. He has had religious education in the Episcopal Church and the wife and child in the Roman Catholic Church. Their story:

Religious preparation prior to marriage involved six one-and-one-half-hour sessions with the priest. The overall view of the priest was negative. To this day my husband remembers how the priest said that he was an "intruder" by marrying a Catholic and how the Catholic faith encourages people to marry someone from their own faith.

Our wedding was a family celebration. Preparation for our child's baptism involved three sessions with our priest (different parish). This priest had a much brighter view and had a positive effect.

Raising a child in a home where one set of grandparents is Episcopalian and the other set is Catholic has some difficulties. During holidays or whenever we visit, we as Catholics must go to our Church for Sunday Mass. If our child wants to go with her grandparents (Episcopalians), she must get to the Catholic Mass too. I have reservations about this but have not deviated from the Catholic teaching. The same goes regarding Communion. If her grandparents (Episcopalians) attend Mass with her, they are unable to partake of Communion due to our differences.

To other couples planning marriage, I feel it is important to discuss before marriage how children will be raised, Catholic or otherwise. My husband has always been very supportive, and has assisted in raising our child Catholic.

Domestic ARC Church D. A fifty-four-year-old Episcopalian, who had religious education, worships regularly in her church. Her Roman Catholic husband received religious instruction in his church and worships there regularly. The children, twenty-eight and twenty-three, were baptized in the Roman Catholic Church and received Catholic religious education. The older worships regularly in the Episcopal Church. The younger does not worship regularly. Their story:

We participated in six weeks "instruction" at a Roman Catholic church. The Roman Catholic clergy were generally "hard liners" with two exceptions. One such presided at the wedding, in which the family was in the wedding party. There was no Mass because of the "mixed marriage."

All Sundays the Roman Catholic husband (and boys) attend Mass. I attend Eucharist. Occasional visits to each others' parish for special events, i.e., baptism (both boys Roman Catholics), confirmation (Roman Catholics), and family celebrations.

Take boys to religious education classes each week. Share lessons. Incorporate Advent and Lenten prayers for meals. Use material from both Roman Catholic and Episcopal Christian education. Celebrate separately on Sundays.

Blessings: respect for each other's differences.

Problems: Sunday morning schedules; birth control restrictions.

Solutions: Accommodate whenever possible. When not possible, always adhere to Roman Catholic requirement (i.e., when traveling, find a Roman Catholic church for Mass and not try to attend separate services).

Unresolved issues: death may be one. We'll respect each other's wishes and put them in writing.

ARC. Go for the "good stuff." Believing is the important issue. There's a lot to be said for the challenge of "being your own person." It's easier to go to one church—but it's not easy at all if it's not what feels real. Respect your own faith—and his. It is a source of great personal strength.

He (as a Roman Catholic) *belongs* to my church. I (as an Episcopalian) am *guest* at his.

Follow guidelines insofar as possible.

Domestic ARC *Church E.* An Episcopalian and his Roman Catholic wife, both seventy-eight, are baptized, educated, and worship regularly in their respective churches. Their two children were baptized Roman Catholic and educated in the Roman Catholic Church. Their story:

Before marriage we agreed each would keep his or her own religious background. We were married by a justice of the peace. After leaving the U.S. military service we were married in a Roman Catholic sacristy with the Episcopalian's family present.

Weekly attendance—at an Episcopal church for husband, and a Roman Catholic church for wife. Daily prayers at meals and night prayers. There is no problem. Husband supports Roman Catholic Church.

Daughter and family attend the Roman Catholic church; the son is not affiliated with either church.

Both agree on all sacraments, but do not agree with shared practice in separate communion.

When necessary we go to either an Anglican or a Roman Catholic church. Both believe that the liturgies of both churches are equal. Wife receives Holy Communion in either church; husband would receive the sacrament of Holy Communion if it were approved in the Roman Catholic Church. No problem with one another's traditions. Both children respect our religious traditions.

Domestic ARC Church F. A fifty-one-year-old baptized Roman Catholic woman received a Roman Catholic religious education and worships regularly in the Roman Catholic Church as does her twenty-four-year-old son. Her fifty-four-year-old husband, baptized in the Episcopal Church, received religious education and worships regularly in the Episcopal Church. Their twenty-three-year-old daughter was baptized and religiously educated in the Roman Catholic Church. They were married in 1964. Their story:

> Our ARC "story" is not very dramatic. We have both remained involved with our respective churches, i.e., CCD instruction, Eucharistic minister, council member for me, and more rigorous time/effort considerations for husband such as several years as senior warden, instructor, lay reader, etc. We respect each other's involvement and don't interfere.
>
> For special occasions such as confirmations, Christmas (when the children were younger), on vacations, we will attend services together. Mostly he comes with me.
>
> At our wedding at my parish church, two Episcopal ministers, my father-in-law and brother-in-law (best man), attended. They were both attired in their clerical outfits, and my father-in-law stood with the Catholic priest as he performed the wedding service.
>
> There really have been no problems due to our religious differences. It would be nice to attend church together though.
>
> My husband has been involved in ecumenical activities (covenant committee) for eight or nine years; I less so, and for a shorter time.

These stories reveal ARC domestic churches as communities in which members share to various degrees the churches of the other. The stories indicate the variety of ways the Episcopalians and Roman Catholics in ARC families receive guidelines on marriage and sharing the Eucharist. These stories also indicate that our churches have not adequately received either the hopes or the pains experienced by ARC families.[12]

12. The issues mentioned in these stories of 1990 are the same as those in *ARC Marriages, A Study of U.S. Couples living Episcopal–Roman Catholic Marriages,* by a joint Standing Committee of The Episcopal Diocesan Ecumenical Officers and The National Association of Diocesan Ecumenical Officers, May 5, 1981. The committee called upon the bishops and their respective agencies for family life and care to be sensitive to the needs raised in their study, and to give new directions in this growing area of our common life in Christ.

Although some ARC spouses have received the church of the other, after twenty-five years of serious dialogue neither of our churches has officially received the other. The human cost of this non-reception, this disunity, is severe. This is true not only for ARC families, but also for the whole human family, which may see in our broken relationship no model of Trinitarian unity, of unity in diversity. It may also be argued that our churches' inability to restore our broken relationship, when we hold as one so many values and sacred memories, is no model for those spouses within each tradition who are called to restore their broken marital relationships rather than to settle for a severed marriage.

Conclusion

To celebrate the joy and to relieve the pain experienced by ARC families, the restoration of full communion is of profound importance. We ask, therefore, to what sacred place will our lay and official pilgrimage bring our two churches in the 1990s? Will the pilgrims, lay and official, journey together or on separate paths? A partial answer may lie in the reception by the official churches of the experiences of ARC families. Our hope is that by probing the words of the official church and hearing the stories of ARC spouses our two churches may advance to the full communion that is "already among us enfleshed in the union of Episcopal and Roman Catholic couples."[13]

A more immediate hope is for our churches to loose the constraints which bind those ARC families who bear witness to the unity which is to come. Our two churches must provide appropriate religious education for families for whose children the first experience of "church" is in the domestic church of an ARC family.

We therefore recommend that our theologies of baptism, Eucharist, church, and marriage be applied to the increasing reality of ecumenical families and in particular to ARC families. More concretely, we ask that the Roman Catholic as well as the Episcopal churches encourage members of ARC families, and in some cases their extended families, to discriminately receive Communion in both churches. We ask that our churches explore a dual membership of full membership in one's own church and an associate membership or partnership in the church of one's spouse for those who are living in ARC domestic churches. We ask that our churches develop baptismal celebrations which reflect the reality of an ARC domestic church. We believe such actions will strengthen the visible sign of ARC unity between our two churches and also relieve the weight of disunity for ARC families.

13. Bishops of Illinois (see note 5), 7.

4

Anglican–Roman Catholic Covenants

Experiencing Unity and Frustration

The parish continues to be the focus of Christian community for most Roman Catholics and Episcopalians. National and international dialogues may argue theological points, and local bishops may, or may not, cooperate at least on some social issues and join in non-Eucharistic worship. At the parochial level, these events sometimes have little impact. Yet over the years contact between the two traditions has moved from a latently suspicious and competitive regard to an implicit realization that the other is an historically and theologically conditioned expression of a shared faith, even though real contact between the two faith communities at the local level varies enormously.

Laity are frequently less tolerant of ecclesiastical divisions than are clergy, because they express their faith and discern the faith of others primarily in practical rather than theological ways. If ecumenical relationships foster greater efficiency in relieving human suffering, they are embraced with enthusiasm. If these relationships are perceived as opportunities for theological chat which are ineffective in terms of lived Christianity, they do not move laypersons to seek involvement.

Those who champion ecumenical discussions and projects frequently complain that they find it difficult to motivate laypersons to participate in these activities. Discouraged, the professional ecumenist (usually someone theologically educated) concludes that ecumenism is dying, that the laity are insular, or that only church professionals have ecumenical yearnings. Yet ties of family, and the need to redress wrong and alleviate suffering, draw many—one is tempted to say most—Christian laypersons into a web of real—but unrecognized—ecumenical activities and relationships.

Impatient with a divided Christendom, Roman Catholics and Episcopalians in some parts of the country have entered into covenants of mutual prayer and activity. Convinced of the incongruity of separation in the face of Christ's prayer "that they may all be one," and recognizing that their baptism in the name of the Holy Trinity commits them to, and incorporates them in, the same Christ, Roman Catholics and Anglicans have established covenant relationships between dioceses, between cathedral churches, between parishes, and even between a parish and a religious house.

Diocesan Covenants

The following diocesan covenants were studied for this report: Connecticut (Episcopal) and Norwich (Roman Catholic), begun June 29, 1980; Milwaukee, begun 1983; Atlanta, begun January 3, 1984; Chicago, begun November 16, 1986; and a state-wide Lutheran–Anglican–Roman Catholic Covenant in Virginia entered upon November 1, 1990.

While articles of covenant vary from place to place, certain commitments appear consistently:

—to pray for one another, by name, both daily in private prayers and regularly in liturgical worship;

—to cooperate in sponsoring retreats and sharing resources for spiritual growth and formation;

—to engage in regular dialogue and/or joint study by clergy and laity throughout the year;

—to sponsor joint educational activities for clergy and laity;[1]

—to consult and cooperate in social action ministries;

—to discuss international and national developments within each communion as well as with the covenant partner(s);

—to share physical facilities whenever feasible.

Most covenanted dioceses also undertake to review the covenant and its effectiveness annually, and to renew it liturgically. Several covenants specifically encourage maintaining the unique traditions of each church and fostering the study of the other tradition. Some pledge to work to remove existing obstacles to greater unity and not to erect new ones.

Other dioceses are working toward covenant, or have established a commitment of intent, for example, Albany, and Rio Grande (Episcopal), Santa Fe (Roman Catholic).

1. Topics include papal encyclicals, church history and teaching, and practical (applied) Christianity.

Parish Covenants

Within dioceses in covenant relationship, and in dioceses not so connected, parish churches have in some places entered into covenant relationships with one another. These parish covenants, like those between
the dioceses, promise:

>—to pray for one another regularly and in public worship;

>—to explore ways of sharing financial resources, facilities, and
>ministry, particularly ministries of education and social action;

>—to invite members of the companion congregation to social,
>educational, and liturgical functions.

Although information has not been available to us on the exact circumstances behind the formation of all these covenants, our general impression is that friendship between the clergy was often a seed, which was
then planted in consultation with vestries/parish councils, and cultivated
by discussions in the two parishes at large. Only when the proposal met
with approval at all these levels did the two parishes agree to enter into
covenant. The experience of those involved has generally been that without active discussion and sympathetic involvement of the laity, the covenant remains, or quickly becomes, a clerical comradeship.

Responses to our inquiry from members of covenanted parishes range
from enthusiastic to discouraged. The commonest observation was that
those—few is implied—who participate in joint activities find the experience very rewarding but that most members of either parish take little
interest in the relationship. Some clergy report a cooling of enthusiasm
in recent years, which they attribute to a perception on the part of Episcopalians that Rome is no longer serious about ecumenism and has gone
back to a "return to Rome" mentality, or that difficult questions at issue, such as authority and abortion, are closed to discussion. Tensions
and therefore coolness exist where there are clergy who have transferred
from one tradition to the other—although lay transfers seem not to raise
the same concerns. The disparity in size between Episcopal (usually small)
and Roman Catholic (usually large) parishes and the resulting different
workloads of the clergy was seen as a difficulty. Episcopal priests sometimes fear being outnumbered.

Broadening an ARC Relationship

In some places an ARC covenant relationship, parochial or diocesan,
has broadened to include Lutherans (LARC) or has become the base of a
local council of several churches. A Lutheran parish, a Roman Catholic

parish, and an Episcopal parish entered a two-year covenant in April 1990 and marked the occasion with a joint procession from church to church, with members carrying blessed baptismal water which was then poured together and shared among all three congregations. In November, 1990, two Roman Catholic dioceses (Arlington and Richmond), three Episcopal dioceses (Virginia, Southern Virginia, and Southwestern Virginia), and the Metropolitan Washington Synod of the Evangelical Lutheran Church in America, jointly entered into a statewide LARC covenant. Six years of statewide LARC conferences, with both clerical and lay participation, preceded the covenant, which received strong episcopal support from bishops of all three judicatories.

Covenants Revisited

Three covenanted parishes in three quite different geographical locations across the country were studied and visited by EDEO–NADEO teams in 1980.[2] A decade later a new EDEO–NADEO Standing Committee attempted to contact these parishes to ascertain how the relationship had endured over the intervening decade and how developments in either tradition— for example, changes of leadership, the ordination of women by Episcopalians and papal statements on the possibility of such ordinations, or the polarization between advocates of pro-life and pro-choice ethical positions—had affected the covenant relationship.

The covenanted parishes studied in 1980 were:

1. Ogden, Utah
   Good Shepherd Episcopal Church
   St. Joseph's Roman Catholic Church

2. Louisville, Kentucky
   A) The Archdiocese of Louisville
      The Diocese of Kentucky
      Christ Church Episcopal Cathedral
      R.C. Cathedral of the Assumption

   B) St. Matthew's Episcopal Church (St. Matthew, Kentucky)
      Holy Trinity Roman Catholic Church (St. Matthew, Kentucky)

   C) St. Luke's Episcopal Church (Anchorage, Kentucky)
      The R.C. Community of the Epiphany (Anchorage, Kentucky)

2. See *A Tale of Three Cities: A Study of U.S. ARC Covenants* (EDEO/NADEO, 1980).

3. Tidewater, Virginia
The Church of the Holy Apostles, a unique parish shared by
a Roman Catholic and an Episcopal community

New information could not be obtained from Utah. The replies from
Kentucky and Virginia follow:

Louisville: The dioceses and cathedral congregations: a new archbishop
has been appointed since the 1980 study, and the diocese was in the process
of seeking an ecumenical officer when contacted. Both Archbishop
Thomas Kelly and the Episcopal ecumenical officer invited the
EDEO–NADEO team to visit Louisville. Once a Roman Catholic ecumenical
officer has been hired, the Episcopal officer anticipates holding a one-
day conference of covenanted parishes "not only for gathering information on the process of the covenants but also for an exchange of practical
information."

The pastor of the Cathedral of the Assumption, less optimistic, reported that "for the last few years our covenant has been stagnant. . . .
In essence it is dormant, waiting for revival." This he attributed not to
a decline of ecumenical-mindedness but to changes in the pastorates and
"major revitalization programs in both places" that were, apparently, not
inclusive of the covenant partner.

St. Matthew, Kentucky: The Episcopal rector replied only when
prodded by a second letter and then admitted to having written an initial
response and "stashed it away in my word processor memory because it
was so negative." Like the cathedrals in Louisville, the two parishes continue to pray for one another and to "do some symbolic things" together,
but the rector characterized the relationship as at a low point. The one
happy exception he pointed to was a joint sponsorship in the summer of
1988 of live-in visits by eight Northern Irish young people, four Protestants and four Roman Catholics. While a good event, the experience could
not, for unspecified reasons, be repeated. The rector was quite frank in
saying:

> I believe that the present state of the Roman Catholic Church dic-
> tates against good ecumenical relationships. I have served as one of
> the ecumenical members of their Archdiocesan Ecumenical Commis-
> sion, as well as being a part of our covenant work for many years,
> and I see the change that has taken place. There is, on the part of
> many of them, a drawing back, a silence, a sense of discomfort, and
> an increasing number of times when they feel it necessary to say, "No,
> we can't do that. . . ." We have talked frankly about such things
> in our committee work. I have made good friends at Holy Trinity,
> our covenant parish, and in the archdiocese, but our working together
> and the friendships have only increased my awareness of how far apart

we still are. . . . I believe there is once again the rise of Roman triumphalism, and what that means ecumenically is the old business that "Ecumenism means, 'Come home to Rome.' "

Asked (as were all the pastors) whether the ordination of women and abortion issues had affected the relationship, the rector replied that women's ordination has not been a factor in the parochial relationship. On the abortion issue he expressed some impatience with "party line" unanimity among Roman Catholics on an issue hotly and agonizingly debated from both ideological sides among his own parishioners.

Finally, in explaining his parishioners' lack of interest in reactivating the covenant, he pointed to their involvement in AIDS work, abortion counselling, Bible study, work with the homeless, and liturgical study, and justified their considerable indifference to a stagnating ecumenism by saying, "I just cannot ask them to give their time to an ecumenical endeavor which shows little progress and some setback."

Anchorage, Kentucky: Both St. Luke's Church and the Church of the Epiphany responded to the inquiry. The Roman Catholic pastor of Epiphany characterized the covenant as "on a scale of one to ten . . . about a six or seven." Several changes in rectors at the Episcopal parish and a difference in their attitudes to the importance of the covenant had, he felt, moved the relationship from active to "almost moribund" to "at least alive and well." He fears that when he is transferred, "it could die without strong Roman leadership." The decision of one rector to leave the Episcopal Church and become a Roman Catholic priest in 1988 "did not help the covenant that much."

The Episcopal congregation he described as "very, very conservative" and very small (400); the Episcopalians oppose the ordination of women, while the Roman Catholic congregation of 3,500 supports it. The Episcopalians "were very upset by the episcopal ordination of Barbara Harris, while we rejoiced." The Episcopal rector concurred by saying that "Epiphany tends to be more liberal than the Vatican on [the issue of women's ordination], and St. Luke's is more conservative than the official position of the Episcopal Church."

The presence of a number of ARC couples within the congregations seems not to have stimulated continued cooperation. Both priests agreed that national and international dialogues and documents have little effect locally, although ARC and ARCIC have been discussed at the archdiocesan level. The Anchorage Presbyterian Church has been drawn into the covenant, forming a three-way relationship. This, in the words of the Episcopal rector, has created a "kind of fascination with the fact of a covenant between Presbyterians and Roman Catholics." The only pulpit exchange, in fact, has been between the Roman Catholics and Presbyterians, although for several years lenten classes have been developed among the three.

The two pastors, apparently having different expectations and levels of zeal, characterized the relationship and its future somewhat differently. The Episcopal rector writes:

> I believe that the covenant here will continue to be important, especially in the way the two congregations view each other. There is a feeling of harmony and good will; the clergy are friends; and a small group of people in each parish intentionally work and pray for the strengthening of this covenant and the unity of the church.

The Catholic pastor warns:

> The biggest caution I have is trying to get "grass-roots" support for ecumenical activity. Laity, for the most part, are not interested in theological questions and problems. They feel that our slowness in Christian unity is a scandal, and they have little patience with it. Intercommunion is happening more and more, with or without permission. Pastors and their attitude will continue to be KEY in the future! Our Archdiocese and the Episcopal diocese have been very helpful and encouraging here, but more leadership is needed on the international level (particularly from the Vatican) before anything significant will happen.

Tidewater, Virginia: The Church of the Holy Apostles in Virginia Beach, Virginia, is unique in being the only fully shared Roman Catholic-Episcopal parish in the country. It was founded after four years of study by a joint committee appointed by Bishop Walter F. Sullivan of the Roman Catholic Diocese of Richmond and Bishop David S. Rose of Southern Virginia. Hoping to meet the needs of a rapidly growing population and to reflect the ecumenical advances between the two communions, the bishops installed co-pastors on All Saints' Day 1977. Each of these two full-time priests was called according to the procedures of his canons and diocese. Thirty households responded to an invitation issued at this service to share in the joint witness of Holy Apostles.

This fledgling ARC community was to model on the parish level the reconciling relationship of sister churches. The ecclesiology of *koinonia*, increasingly the foundation of Anglican–Roman Catholic, and other, ecumenical documents, was here to be lived out: two bishops shared *episcopé*, two priests provided pastoral care; an Episcopal vestry and a Catholic parish council together developed a constitution which was approved by the bishops, and together when possible, and separately when necessary, they provided lay leadership for the new community. In this they follow the Lund Principle of doing everything together except when "deep differences of conviction compel them to act separately."[3]

3. The so-called Lund Principle is a statement enunciated by the Conference on Faith and Order of the World Council of Churches, meeting in 1962 in Lund, Sweden.

Although Sunday Eucharists are celebrated separately, members work together to plan liturgy, develop a formation program and execute social ministry. Christian education is centered on adults, who then provide primary Christian formation for their children, focused on the liturgical year, and drawn from the common lectionary. Social outreach, prompted by worship and informed by catechetics, presents to those outside the church a model of Christian unity in mission "so that the world may believe." Festivals and social events bring Catholics and Episcopalians together in what the first Catholic pastor, Fr. Ray Barton, calls "the joy and unity of the parish [made] manifest."

Conclusion

This random sampling of covenant relationships between Anglican and Roman Catholics at both diocesan and parochial levels leads to several conclusions, some of which appear to contradict others.

In dioceses and archdioceses where Roman Catholic and Episcopal bishops actively collaborate and who themselves promote covenant cooperation, the clergy and the laity—by and large—see the relationship as an important opportunity for Christian growth. In those places where the chief pastors tolerate but do not show commitment to covenant, ecumenically-minded clergy find themselves uncomfortably caught between an indifferent laity and a reluctant bishop. It is not surprising, therefore, that in these places lay persons of both traditions work and socialize with each other, but rarely see their contacts as in any way ecumenical.[4]

The principle has been affirmed and commended by the Lambeth Conference of Anglican Bishops (1968) and affirmed by the General Convention of the Episcopal Church, USA (1976). The statement reads in part: "A faith in the one Church of Christ which is not implemented by acts of obedience is dead. There are truths about the nature of God and His Church which will remain for ever closed to us unless we act together in obedience to the unity which is already ours. We would, therefore, earnestly request our Churches to consider whether they are doing all they ought to do to manifest the oneness of the people of God. Should not our Churches ask themselves whether they are showing sufficient eagerness to enter into conversation with other Churches and whether they should not act together in all matters except those in which deep difference of conviction compel them to act separately?"

4. The EDEO/NADEO Standing Committee expresses its appreciation to the following persons whose cooperation made this report possible: Rev. Ray Barton, Rev. Charles K. Blanck, Rev. Bruce H. Cooke, Rev. Robert P. Coval, Sr. Therese Dion, S.S.D., Rev. Ernest R. Falardeau, S.S.S., Rev. Joseph T. Graffis, Rev. Jerome M. Hudziak, Phoebe (Mrs. Ebbe) Hoff, Rev. Richard H. Humke, Right Rev. Thomas C. Kelly, O.P., Rev. Ronald Knott, Rev. J. Raymond Lord, Rev. Canon Henry Male, Anne C. Shire, the Ven. Charles B. Tachau, Rev. Warren Tanghe, Rev. Michael K. Thompson, Rt. Rev. Roger White, Rev. John R. Williams.

Sample Covenants

A DIOCESAN COVENANT

In the name of the Father, the Son, and the Holy Spirit.

Believing in the will of the Lord Jesus Christ that we "all may be one," recognizing our common baptism in the name of the Trinity, and encouraged by the local desire of our people in these two dioceses, we, Joseph Cardinal Bernardin and Bishop James W. Montgomery, in the name of these our people, solemnly and reverently enter into this Covenant and pledge:

1. To strive for the removal of any existing obstacle to union while supporting and preserving the traditions of each other—Anglican and Roman Catholic—according to the mandate of the Gospel.

2. To place no impediment to the cause of unity.

3. To pray for each other daily, and to encourage our people to do the same for their local churches of our two communions.

4. To ask our local congregations to include in our liturgies petitions for greater unity in our local churches.

5. To share the spiritual resources of our two communions in a context of common prayer, reflection and times of retreat.

6. To offer and to share our facilities and resources on the parish and diocesan levels.

7. To commit ourselves, where appropriate, to joint planning of some programs of our churches.

8. To work together for social justice as essential to Gospel witness.

9. To further embody this diocesan covenant by encouraging existing parish covenants and by enabling parishes to establish new ones.

10. To ask that parishioners of our respective communions participate in regularly scheduled joint prayer services in witness of the Covenant.

11. To pursue a continuing dialogue between our dioceses in the spirit of the international and national dialogue, promoting better understanding.

12. To share and discuss decisions made at various levels in our churches, namely, national conferences of Bishops, conventions, and councils.

We dedicate ourselves to these objectives and ask the blessing of our loving God on this Covenant that we may be faithful to it to His Honor and Glory.

November 16, 1986

A PARISH COVENANT

In the name of the Father and of the Son and of the Holy Spirit.

WHEREAS it is the will of the founder of the Christian Religion "that they all may be one";

WHEREAS the highest leadership of the Roman Catholic and Anglican Churches have expressed a desire for reunion of Christian Churches;

WHEREAS the theologians of these Churches are meeting to solve the theological problems involved in reunion;

WHEREAS the Episcopal Bishop of Milwaukee and the Roman Catholic Archbishop of Milwaukee have expressed a desire that the parishes in their diocese prepare themselves for this reunion;

WHEREAS the people of St. Peter's Episcopal Church and St. Rita's Roman Catholic Church both in the City of West Allis and the State of Wisconsin are conscious of the Will of Jesus Christ and the desire of their respective Churches for reunion.

WE HEREBY ENTER INTO THIS COVENANT:

WE SOLEMNLY PLEDGE:

1. TO place no impediment in the way of reunion.

2. TO include in all of our liturgies a petition to God for the reunion of our Churches.

3. TO include in all our liturgies a prayer for each other.

4. TO share as far as is feasible our facilities.

5. TO make available to each other the programs sponsored by the individual congregation.

6. TO periodically gather together for prayer services.

7. TO work together for social justice and the Common Good.

8. TO sponsor joint social events.

WE PLEDGE OURSELVES TO THESE OBJECTIVES AND ASK THE BLESSING OF ALMIGHTY GOD ON THESE COVENANTS THAT THEY MIGHT BE FAITHFUL TO THEM TO HIS HONOR AND GLORY.

(1973)

A State-wide Lutheran/Anglican/Roman Catholic Covenant

PREAMBLE

We Bishops are witnesses to two powerful experiences in our time which have impelled Lutherans, Episcopalians and Roman Catholics toward church unity: the Ecumenical Movement and the Second Vatican Council. The Holy Spirit continues to use the graced events to enlighten and form God's people as we approach the Third Millennium.

Unity is a Gospel imperative for the churches, not simply an option. We are mindful that our Lord and Savior, Jesus Christ, the night before he died prayed: ". . . that they may all be one, Father! May they be in us, just as you are in me and I am in you. May they be one, so that the world will believe that you sent me. I gave them the same glory you gave me, so that they may be one, just as you and I are one: I in them and you in me, so that they may be completely one, in order that the world may know that you sent me and that you love them as you love me" (Jn. 17:21-23). The psalmist, too, reminds us: "How wonderful it is, how pleasant, for God's people to live together in harmony" (Psalm 133).

Furthermore, it is our responsibility to "make every effort to preserve the unity which has the Spirit as its origin and peace as its binding force" because: "There is but one Body and one Spirit, . . . just as there is one Lord, one faith, one baptism; one God and Father of all, who is over all, and works through all and is all" (Eph. 4:4-6).

We celebrate the faithful initiative of our church leaders, past and present, in fostering church unity. In our roles as pastoral leaders, we welcome Pope John Paul II's and Archbishop Runcie's challenge: "Once more, then, we call on the bishops, clergy, and faithful people . . . in every country, diocese, and parish in which our faithful live side by side. We urge them all to pray for this work and to adopt every possible means of furthering it through their collaboration, in deepening their allegiance to Christ and in witnessing to him before the world. Only by such collaboration and prayer can the memory of past enmities be healed and our past antagonisms overcome."

In Virginia, we experience the call to full communion in various collaborative efforts among our three traditions: in particular, through the annual statewide Lutheran, Anglican, Roman Catholic (LARC) Conference, at regional LARC events for the Week of Prayer for Christian Unity, and in local parish initiatives. We hear this call also in the Anglican–Roman Catholic Commission's (ARCIC's) *Final Report,* in the Lutheran–Roman Catholic document, *Facing Unity,* in the Lutheran–Episcopal *Niagara Report*, and, in the United States, in *The Agreement.* In these joint undertakings our divisions are being healed and we become attuned to the Spirit who makes us one.

DECLARATION

We recognize that it is the Holy Spirit who bestows unity. The same Spirit calls us to uncover convergences and to achieve consensus so that we can advance toward the goal of unity willed by Christ. Through conversion, this shared commitment opens us to new possibilities under the guidance of God's Spirit as we seek to provide an effective expression of God's love in Christ.

Two decades of dialogues have led our three traditions to establish full communion as our mutual goal. We understand that we will pursue this goal in a rich variety of ways which are consistent with the Gospel and the ordering of our three traditions.

We desire to do all things together which existing agreements permit and to place no impediment to the cause of unity.

THEREFORE, relying on the faithful love of the Triune God, we commit ourselves to celebrate the unity already achieved through years of Lutheran–Anglican–Roman Catholic conversations and to strengthen the visible unity of the Body of Christ in Virginia.

A CALL INTO COVENANT

The unity of the church is the gift of the Spirit and a task of the church. We hereby CALL INTO COVENANT respective Synods and Dioceses and COMMIT OURSELVES to the following actions. In behalf of the unity of the church, WE WILL:

1. pray for each other, particularly at the principal Sunday celebration;

2. sponsor seasonal prayer services, especially during the Week of Prayer for Christian Unity;

3. encourage shared lectionary studies;

4. promote pulpit exchanges in accord with the respective guidelines of each tradition;

5. encourage cooperation among member churches in providing pre-marital preparation for ecumenical marriages;

6. encourage shared religious formational and educational events, e.g., youth ministry, vacation Bible school, living room dialogue;

7. develop joint efforts in evangelism and social justice;

8. develop covenants among our congregations, institutions and chaplaincies;

9. support statewide, regional and local LARC Conferences, and establish annually a joint meeting of our ecumenical bodies;

10. encourage each diocese and synod to develop supportive prayer services and covenanting models for its congregations through their respective ecumenical and liturgical committees;

11. urge congregations to study the existing dialogues among our churches;

12. develop covenants among schools and academies for shared programs;

13. ask congregations to develop and reflect on their cooperative ministries to discover areas of convergence among our three churches;

14. sponsor shared retreats and formational events for clergy and parish leadership;

15. develop campus ministry covenants among Catholic Campus Ministry, Canterbury Association, and Lutheran Student Union;

16. seek ways to coordinate program and planning at the district/synodical/diocesan level;

17. collaborate at the judicatory level on justice issues and social concerns;

18. review and evaluate this Covenant annually at a meeting of the State LARC Committee representatives with Bishops;

19. establish goals annually which advance this Covenant;

20. celebrate the renewal of this Covenant annually at the statewide LARC Conference.

May the Holy Spirit, who has brought us to this moment of covenanting, bring us to ever deepening levels of unity; To this end we affix our names and recommend it to our respective judicatories.

November 1, 1990

EPISCOPÉ
AND
COMMUNITY

5

Bishops

Focus or Failure

The purpose of all Christian ministry is to build up the church as a communion. No other model could be more basic to the notion of the Church or more faithful to the New Testament understanding of the Church. *The Final Report* of the first Anglican/Roman Catholic Consultation recognizes this when it states that "all ministries are used by the Holy Spirit for the building up of the Church to be this reconciling community for the glory of God and the salvation of men."[1]

The section of *The Final Report* that deals with ministry and ordination considers an essential element of ordained ministry to be one of responsibility for oversight. This oversight was never intended to be an exercise of worldly power or domination; it was intended to focus the unity of the church as a community in fidelity to the Gospel and Christian doctrine. The ordained ministry was intended to reflect Jesus as the Good Shepherd, the one who calls some of his disciples to become fishers of people. It is an office of service to the wider membership of the church, and those who hold the office of bishop are expected to animate and guide the Christian community in its life of faith and service, in its calling "to declare the wonderful deeds" of God in Christ (1 Pet 2:9). Nonetheless, the ordained ministry is not simply an extension of the common priesthood of all Christians. It "belongs to another realm of the gifts of the Spirit" as ARCIC I notes.[2]

ARCIC I makes clear for Anglicans and Roman Catholics that bishops (*episcopoi*) are entrusted with special oversight (*episcopé*) of the local church. As a body, bishops are called to maintain the church as a communion (*koinonia*) of churches united in faith and in holiness of life. The unity of the church is symbolized and realized in a significant way through the instrumentality of this office. By it we are kept in continuity with the

1. *The Final Report,* Statement on Ministry and Ordination (1973) 5.
2. *Ibid.,* 12.

church stretching back to the apostolic age—in this respect we often refer to bishops as being in apostolic succession. Our specific concern in this section is to look at some instances where episcopal oversight has not been exercised with sufficient respect for the significance of the office of bishop. Such instances have repercussions affecting Anglicans and Roman Catholics in their growth into full visible unity. Our concern for the exercise of episcopal authority is in no way meant to diminish other ministries in the church or treat them as second-rate ministries. All ministry is essential to the life and mission of the church.

In presuming Anglican and Roman Catholic agreement on the significance of bishops in the church's faith and order, we do not want to give the impression that our desire for unity is not for the unity of all Christian churches. Though we pay special attention to Anglican–Roman Catholic concern over the exercise of *episcopé*, we wish to respect differences which arise over the history, the nature and function of this office in other churches as well as in our own. In locating *episcopé* in a single office holder, the bishop (*episcopos*), we do not intend to undervalue the fact of a consensus with other Christians that oversight or supervision has been in the church from the very beginning to maintain the church as a community devoted to the teaching of the apostles, communion, the breaking of the bread and the prayers, after the pattern of Acts 2:42.

Anglicans and Roman Catholics understand in principle that the ministry of bishops is to be exercised in concert with other ministries and services in the church. And from time to time, bishops exercise their ministry in a collegial way, e.g., through councils, synods, the meeting of primates, or episcopal conferences. Bishops represent the wider church in their own churches since their task is to strengthen the church as a communion of communions. In such a joint exercise of episcopacy, they do more than symbolize the unity of the church, they realize it as well, and act to ensure the church's growth in communion or fellowship. Yet we must be clear. The bishops are not alone in this. They act in concert with other official officeholders and the membership of the church in general, for all members of the church are charged with responsibility for perfecting the credibility and visibility of the church's witness as a communion of love and loving service for the whole world. The Meissen Report of 1988 summarizes this: "We acknowledge that personal and collegial oversight (*episkopé*) is embodied and exercised in our churches in a variety of forms, episcopal and non-episcopal, as a visible sign of the Church's unity and continuity in apostolic life, mission and ministry."[3]

3. The Meissen Report is a statement issued by the Church of England and the Federation of Evangelical Churches in the German Democratic Republic and the Evangelical Church in Germany in the Federal Republic of Germany. Issued in 1988 prior to the reunification of Germany, it can be obtained from the Board of Mission and Unity, Church House, Great Smith Street, London SW1P 3NZ, United Kingdom.

Sources of Tension

We are aware that in the course of the church's history changing circumstances and developments have affected the role of the bishop in the church. In our two churches there has been tension, and often a lack of balance, between the governing role of the bishop and his role as a teacher of the faith. There have been times when the governing authority has far outweighed the teaching authority. Tension and imbalance in this respect continue to disturb our two churches internally and in their ecumenical relationship. The primacy of the bishop of Rome in respect to other bishops continues to exacerbate suspicions that the proper authority of a local bishop can be set aside, that conferences of bishops carry no weight, and that other instances of collective episcopal gatherings are more consultative than determinative. We also share a concern over the invasion of a bishop's jurisdiction by a bishop from another jurisdiction. There is also the ongoing tension in the bishop who must present himself both as a teacher of the faith and as a theologian capable of theological reasoning and speculation. This tension logically suggests a tension in those who function in the church as professional theologians, between what they owe to their own conscience and to legitimate teaching authority in the church.

To illustrate these tensions which affect Anglican–Roman Catholic relations we have selected four cases because they are still fresh in many minds. First, to illustrate the tension between the centralized jurisdiction of the Vatican, representing the bishop of Rome, and a diocesan bishop, we present the "Hunthausen case" where the jurisdiction of a diocesan bishop was divided, the proper diocesan bishop was left with only partial jurisdiction, and was subjected to further investigation of his policies and positions. Second, we look at the case where the bishop of London undertook the administration of sacraments in an Episcopalian diocese in the United States without the granting of jurisdiction by the proper diocesan bishop. This is the "Broken Arrow" case. Next, we look at the controversy aroused by the bishop of Durham, a theologian as well as a diocesan bishop, where his role as teacher of the faith seemed to be jeopardized when he speculated theologically on such doctrines as the virgin birth and the resurrection. We refer to this as the "David Jenkins" case. Finally, we introduce the "Charles Curran" case to show the tension which can arise so easily between the professional theologian and the teaching authority of the church. This tension occurs when episcopal authority sets a limit to theological speculation and moral teaching and the theologian claims academic freedom for his speculation and theological opinion.

Before treating each of these cases in some detail, we must speak of the role of the bishop in the church and the function of oversight in the community of faith. Anglicans may well feel that Roman Catholics place too much emphasis on the bishop as supreme judge and lawgiver in all that affects life in the church and in church policy. Roman Catholics may well be concerned that Anglicans tend to diminish the office of bishop, making the bishop simply one more teacher or administrator in the church. We have no wish to caricature either side. We need a bishop who teaches with a special mandate and exercises an effective authority of oversight or *episcopé*. Failure to get the right balance has led to reactions and reservations over the precise nature and function of the office of bishop in the church as these magnify differences between our two churches. We hope this treatment of the subject is faithful to the measure of agreement reached in our two churches thus far in our renewed relationship. By contrast, the case histories will demonstrate the ongoing need in both our churches to ensure that our theory is matched by the practice of authentic oversight.

6

Oversight

Suppression or Support

Let us focus on *episcopé,* a teaching office in the church. It is important for both our churches to take seriously what ARCIC I says: "Since the ordained ministers are ministers of the Gospel, every facet of their oversight is linked with the word of God. In the original mission and witness recorded in Holy Scripture lies the source and ground of their preaching and authority."[1] This teaching office accounts for the role of oversight which in both our traditions has been associated with the office of bishop. Priests cooperate in this ministry of bishop in a special way by virtue of their ordination. Oversight has to be specified and particularized to ensure sound teaching and fidelity to the Gospel.

The function of oversight is more than a service which ensures the unity of the church as some kind of loose network or federation of churches. It testifies to the unity of the Church as the Body of Christ, enabling it to discharge its responsibility for communicating the word of God for the life of the world. All this has implications for the future of the Anglican and Roman Catholic communions in the context of a new relationship. While we are in substantial agreement on the role of the bishop, there remain differences about the exercise of the episcopal office. Our purpose here is not to stress differences but to indicate the convergence and development in this important area of church life.

Models of Episcopé

It is safe to say that we interpret the function of oversight according to the way we conceptualize the church. The principal theological model in the Roman Catholic Church for a very long time was that of an institu-

1. *The Final Report* "Ministry and Ordination," n. 10. See also "Elucidations," n. 4.

tion with rigorous juridic overtones. An emphasis on the authoritarian exercise of the office of bishop created a division between the clergy and laity.[2] With the reform and renewal of its ecclesiology at Vatican Council II, it discovered a more basic model with a very long tradition, the church as a communion. This model is attractive and effective to Anglicans and now serves as the basis for a dialogue between our two churches.[3]

But Vatican II did not entirely resolve the tension between the church as institution and the church as communion. Since the church is both, the tension is built in and the question is, how creative is the tension in the life and mission of the church? Anglicans must ask the same question. Both churches must make this tension in their respective churches creative. Here our aim is to throw light on the teaching function of the episcopal office when these two ecclesial models are set side by side.[4] The institutional model tends toward the centralization of teaching authority; the communion model favors a greater spread or dispersal of this authority. We can also say that the institutional model emphasizes primacy while the communion model underlines collegiality in the exercise of the teaching office, but neither eliminates the need for the other. Of course, it remains a matter of how each of our two churches understands primacy and collegiality here and now.

Vatican Council II, especially in the documents *Lumen Gentium* and *Dei Verbum,* envisages the church as a community wherein the whole people of God is served by the oversight and teaching of the ordained ministry rather than by a hierarchy with exclusive claims to grace of office and sound teaching, claims which render most members of the church redundant. Anglicans feel more comfortable with the notion of dispersed authority in a church which has had to bring together in its life two strong currents of ecclesial life, viz. the Catholic and reformed traditions. At the institution level of Anglican life this dispersed authority is handled by the

2. Cf. John P. Boyle, "The Rights and Responsibilities of Bishops: A Theological Perspective," *Report of the Joint Committee of the Canon Law Society of American and the Catholic Theological Society of America: Cooperation Between Theologians and the Ecclesiastical Magisterium,* ed. Leo J. Donovan (Washington: The Catholic University of America, 1982) 12–16.

3. ARCIC II issued its agreed statement on this subject in 1991, *Church as Communion.* Aspects of this paper written prior to the agreed statement are further substantiated by it: The New Testament word *koinonia* may be used interchangeably with the word communion or fellowship; *episcopé* (which is used extensively in this paper) may be used interchangeably with the term oversight. Their relationship, the subject of this chapter, is stressed in *Church as Communion,* see esp. nn. 19, 32, 33, 39, and 45.

4. See Ladislas Örsy, *The Church: Learning and Teaching* (Wilmington: Michael Glazier, Inc., 1987) 130–131; Emmanuel Sullivan, "Koinonia As A Meta-Model For Future Church Unity," *Ecumenical Trends* 18:1 (January 1989) 1–8, and the Lutheran And Anglican Responses Following.

interaction of the archbishop of Canterbury, the Primates Meeting, the Anglican Consultative Council, and the Lambeth Conference. At the communion level of Anglican life, this may be best expressed in the words of the Lambeth Conference of 1948:

> [Authority] is distributed among Scripture, Tradition, Creeds, the Ministry of the Word and Sacraments, the witness of the Saints, and the *consensus fidelium,* which is the continuing experience of the Holy Spirit through His faithful people in the Church. It is thus a dispersed rather than a centralized authority having many elements which combine, interact and check each other.[5]

The synodical form of government adopted by the Church of England, and in its general form the government throughout the Anglican communion, reflects the concept of dispersed authority. Attempts at more synodical, conciliar, and collegial forms of government in the Roman Catholic Church remain principally in the realm of bishops and clerics, which reflects a more centralized view of authority in the Church. Both churches will have to live with such differences, though both will have to come to terms with authority both in its central and dispersed forms if unity is to be achieved. In the meantime both Anglicans and Roman Catholics will have to monitor one another as to the effectiveness of such praxis and polity in strengthening the church in its inner life and in its mission to the world.

What does this mean for bishops? Without prejudice to the unique charism of their teaching office, bishops are learning to discern through more careful listening how to serve the needs of the church. They too can learn from the skilled reflections and explanations of theologians who also serve the Gospel and seek to make it relevant for Christian life. Not least, they are subject to learning from the experience of God's people at large, the faithful members of the church. To understand how authentic *episcopé* synthesizes the dialectic of learning and teaching, we must reflect on the teaching office of the bishop in its contemporary development, the meaning of collaboration with other bishops, the interaction of bishops and theologians, and the meaning of pastoral care.

Episcopé: Contemporary Development

Bishops in their own dioceses are teachers endowed with authority to preach the faith and encourage its practice. They are also charged to ward

---

5. "The Meaning and Unity of the Anglican Communion: Lambeth 1948" in Stephen W. Sykes, ed., *Authority in the Anglican Communion* (Toronto: Anglican Book Centre, 1987) 285.

off errors threatening the flock (as in 1 Tim 4:1-4). Bishops are to teach in communion with one another. In the case of the Roman communion, this is highlighted by the communion of bishops with the bishop of Rome. Here Gospel truth is at stake, and the truth of revelation entailed, but there are large areas where theological speculation is open to opinion and often dissent. Where there is dissent the pastoral concern of bishops must be respected, and their decisions received with respect and fidelity. Roman Catholics refer to this as *obsequium,* religious assent which leaves the issue an open question in which conscience must be formed in such a way that the judgment of religious authority is taken into account.

Individual bishops are not infallible. The office of an individual bishop can be described as pastoral, authoritative yet fallible. As pastoral this teaching function of a bishop differs from that of an academic professor of theology. As authoritative it is conditioned and limited to matters of faith and Christian living. As fallible it means that a bishop cannot impose a belief or theological opinion as obligatory when in fact such a belief or opinion is a matter of open and free discussion in the church. When this exercise of *episcopé* is seen within the *koinonia* model of the church, the office is respected for its service to the community of faith. As the Anglican theologian K. S. Chittleborough says: "The personal oversight of a diocesan bishop must go hand in hand with the corporate responsibility shared by bishop, presbyters, deacons, and lay people together. The overlapping authority of the bishop and the bishop-in-synod ensures this. What is said in the Lima Document about personal, collegial, and communion dimensions of oversight exactly describes the Anglican experience."[6] In this context special reference and attention must be made and paid to the relationship between bishop and theologian.

Episcopé: A Work of Collaboration

Here we have to talk about bishops acting in concert. Anglicans may have some difficulty with the heavy use of Roman Catholic theological idiom in such a discussion. Whatever the idiomatic usage, bishops do function as a teaching body or college. The ARCIC statement of 1976, "Authority in the Church I," says that "bishops are collectively responsible for defending and interpreting the apostolic faith."[7] In this context our churches are in dialogue over the issue of how conciliarity and primacy

---

6. See K. S. Chittleborough, "Towards A Theology and Practice of the Bishop-in-Synod" in Sykes, *Authority,* 147–1489. A Roman Catholic point of view on this aspect of *episcopé* can be found in *Lumen Gentium* 3:25-29.

7. *The Final Report,* "Authority in the Church I," n. 20.

genuinely express *episcopé* and build up the church as an effective communion of love, witness, and mission. Yet difficulties do arise, and ARCIC I in its *The Final Report* is at hand to help:

> Although primacy and conciliarity are complementary elements of *episcopé* it has often happened that one has been emphasized at the expense of the other, even to the point of serious imbalance. When churches have been separated from one another, this danger has been increased. The *koinonia* of the churches requires that a proper balance be preserved between the two with the responsible participation of the whole people of God.[8]

Anglicans may be forgiven for feeling slightly more virtuous in getting the "proper balance" than Roman Catholics. On the Anglican side collegiality allows bishops to confer among themselves on occasions such as the Primates Meeting and the Lambeth Conference. It is understood that such conferences have no juridical force or power to make official pronouncements or decisions binding on the churches of the communion, and much less, demand *obsequium* or religious assent from members of the church. Yet they are no charade. There is real consultation and discernment in the process. Moreover, while it is true that the synodal form of government in the Church of England, as exercised through the General Synod, is relatively recent (1970), other Anglican churches not dependent on the crown and parliament introduced synodal government at an early date. Yet even in the Church of England it was presumed that lay members in the House of Commons were lay churchmen whose proper activity would balance the deliberations of bishops in the House of Lords and in other consistories.

Perhaps the best way to understand *episcopé* from a distinctive Anglican point of view is to understand the expression that describes this role of oversight as the "bishop(s)-in-synod." In the Anglican view this does not reduce *episcopé* to a merely honorary function. *Episcopé* is exercised by the bishop in such a way that he or she is clearly part of the overall decision-making, decision-reaching process. The bishop is one who serves the whole church. The bishop of a diocese is elected by clergy and laity, while the synod of a diocese is not the diocese but the instrument whereby the diocese exercises oversight with the bishop. The bishop is "the source and centre of our Order" and he or she wields authority "by virtue of his divine commission and in synodical association with his clergy and laity. . . ."[9] Such oversight is believed to reflect *episcopé* according to the mind and example of Christ. It is a gift of the Holy Spirit for the whole

8. *Ibid*, n. 22.
9. See Chittleborough, "Towards" in Sykes, *Authority,* 149. See also *Authority,* 16.

church and involves the practice of "collegiality" at various levels, so that the bishop shares this oversight with the synod, with other Anglican bishops, and beyond.[10] Roman Catholics have to be aware of too facile a use of a term like *magisterium* in seeking points of agreement between Anglicans and Roman Catholics.[11] From what has just been said, we see clearly that the style and mandate of the bishop as teacher have been interpreted in different ways in the understanding and praxis of this office.

Roman Catholics specify the teaching function of the church in terms of fallibility and infallibility, which we have mentioned with reference to individual bishops. When we come to the conciliar or collaborative exercise of *episcopé* where the teaching role is emphasized, we get into the language of infallibility. Anglicans have difficulty with this and prefer the language of indefectibility. To use the language of infallibility can only mean that the church as a whole is protected from error in essential matters, and with reference to an ecclesiastical office holder such as the bishop of Rome, it means preservation from error in the exercise of his particular charism as teacher of the faith. This is not simply a matter of preference; we must consider infallibility in relation to the question of how *episcopé* safeguards and teaches the way and truth of Christ through the indwelling of the Holy Spirit in the church. Those who favor "indefectibility" express confidence that the Holy Spirit can enable the church to fulfill its mission without giving up their conviction that "the powers of death shall not prevail against it." Those who favor infallibility believe that *episcope* involves a special gift enabling bishops to speak together in such a way that the church is preserved in Christ's truth and in fidelity to the Gospel.[12] *The Final Report* of ARCIC I devotes two sections to this question of authority in the church. While the report points to convergence on the subject, Anglicans and Roman Catholics continue to be so divided that we are unable to speak of consensus or substantial agreement. Both churches, however, are concerned about a teaching authority necessary and effective in the church because some form of collaborative or conciliar oversight is part of the praxis of both our churches.

Such collaborative *episcopé* or oversight developed gradually in the church. Before any theoretical statement of doctrine was worked out there was the practical necessity of dealing with dissensions and unorthodox teachings. Consequently, synods or councils such as the one convened in Jerusalem and recorded in Acts 15 were deemed necessary for the unity

10. See Chittleborough, "Towards," 148–149.

11. See Francis A. Sullivan, *Magisterium: Teaching Authority in the Catholic Church* (New York: Paulist Press, 1983).

12. See Arthur A. Vogel, "Christ's Authority and Ours," *Ecumenical Trends,* 9:10 (November, 1980) 149–156. A letter to the editor in a subsequent issue of *ET,* 10:3 (March 1981) 48, indicates my preference for infallibility over indefectibility.

of faith and practice. Local synods led to larger ones which were later called "ecumenical councils." Ladislas Örsy[13] says that "behind this evolution, there was, no doubt, the conviction that the Spirit of the Lord would always be with the community, and protect it from falsehood. But if the synods could mislead the Church, there would be no protection—which was unthinkable." It was, as he notes, out of "such existential considerations, the doctrine of 'assistance' of the Spirit developed." Out of this came the notion of collaborative *episcopé* which assured the church of authentic teaching—authentic in two ways, viz. official teaching which is subject to correction and subject to reformation, and teaching which confirms a particular doctrine as an integral part of God's revelation. This development found its way into Canon 753 of the new Code of Canon Law for the Western Latin Church:

> Although they do not enjoy infallible teaching authority, the bishops in communion with the head and members of the college, whether as individuals or gathered in conferences of bishops or in particular councils, are authentic teachers and instructors of the faith for the faithful entrusted to their care; the faithful must adhere (*adhaerere tenentur*) to the authentic teaching of their own bishops with a religious assent of soul (*religioso animi obsequio*).

And Canon 749, 2 again refers to this development of collaborative ministry and teaching:

> The college of bishops also possesses infallible teaching authority when the bishops exercise their teaching office gathered together in an ecumenical council when, as teachers and judges of faith and morals, they declare that for the universal Church a doctrine of faith or morals must be definitively held; they also exercise it scattered throughout the world but united in a bond of communion among themselves and with the successor of Peter when together with that same Roman Pontiff in their capacity as authentic teachers of faith and morals, they agree on an opinion to be held as definitive.

From this it seems fairly clear that in Roman Catholic thinking there are relatively few instances where infallible teaching is clearly established and defined. There are many more instances where authentic teaching is pertinent to a particular time and situation but subject to future revision and fresh thinking. Such an exercise in authentic teaching helps us to understand how *episcopé* relates to pastoral care.

---

13. See *The Church*, 36–38.

Episcopé as Pastoral Care

Pastoral care is about people in their experience and culture as they grow toward an ever deeper awareness and commitment to life in Christ as members of his body the church. The laity ought to be the principal concern of those ordained to the pastoral offices of bishop, priest, and deacon. The relationship between ordained and lay members of the church is a two-way relationship. "In such teaching situations, the educational level of the community matters a great deal. A well informed laity can direct the attention of the episcopate to current problems, they can help the bishops formulate the questions correctly before an answer is attempted; more importantly, when the official response is given, they can evaluate it."[14] This is not simply a democratic procedure. Pastoral care is real only when it evokes some response in the faithful membership of the church. The strong sense of faith in faithful members of our churches is often referred to by theologians as the *sensus fidei* and can be described as a supernatural instinct for true faith. It is a gift of the Holy Spirit, a grace bestowed on the whole church, ordained and lay.

Such faith enables the faithful to recognize the teaching authority and give an ungrudging response. This response may well be vigorous, it may be delayed, but it should not be purely passive. It is essential for discerning true faith. Vatican II in its Dogmatic Constitution on the Church[15] details the effects of this instinct for right faith which the Holy Spirit gives to all members of the church who are open to receive it: (1) the teaching is accepted as God's word, (2) it gives an assurance that this is the faith handed on through the ages (viz. tradition), (3) such teaching allows deeper and more accurate insights into the faith, and (4) it applies faith more thoroughly to life situations.

If we are to summarize what is meant by pastoral care, we can say that it means encouraging and assisting more and more members of the church toward maturity as Christians. It means a development of the *sensus fidei,* the instinct for true faith in all the faithful. If we are to appreciate the practical meaning of all this, we must reflect on the Anglican experience which insists on a pastoral role for all members of the church. Anglican understanding of pastoral care requires that laity not be marginalized or made peripheral at this dimension of church life. We have to be careful how we use the image of shepherd and sheep. All Christians have a shepherding role in the church's mission in the world. K. S. Chittleborough states the Anglican position in this regard:

> The *sensus fidelium* in Anglicanism should not be understood as unanimity in the sense of everyone being exactly of the same opin-

14. Örsy, 42–44.
15. See *Lumen Gentium,* 12.

ion, nor is it shown by majority vote in Synod. Synods are not parliamentary democracies, although many parliamentary rules of business procedure have been adopted. Rather . . . consensus government emerges with time, patience, and often costly love which is willing to defer to the common mind even when it has not yet emerged, and when it is "genuinely free."[16]

Episcopé and Theology

We cannot escape the conclusion that *episcopé* or oversight is a teaching and preaching office in the church. Yet we can not unfairly say that bishops have all too often appeared to the public as administrators rather than teachers and preachers of the word of God. Bishops write pastoral letters, and occasionally preach or give a lecture, but they rely heavily on the work of theologians and other trained personnel. This is not a bad thing, and in today's world it ought to be expected. The Anglican experience, particularly in the Church of England, has been conditioned in no small part by the influence of academic theologians. This has created a more open situation and allowed a proliferation of differences of opinion, often to the point of serious division among Anglicans. Differences raised to the level of division are dangerous to the life and witness of the church as a reconciled and reconciling Body of Christ. As Edward Norman has noted, "public commentary has come to see the Church [of England] as divided between 'liberals' . . . and 'traditionalists.' "[17] Since Vatican II this situation has become increasingly common in the Roman Catholic Church. Of course the primary task of a bishop is to maintain the tradition of faith delivered to the saints.[18] Both Anglicans and Roman Catholics know that it is often easier said than done.

Having pointed to this tension between bishop and theologian as a problem for both Anglicans and Roman Catholics, we would be unfair to highlight it in such a way that the two functions come to be seen as radically incompatible. Collaboration between bishops and theologians is both inevitable and desirable. It is a matter of history that the term *magisterium* has been used in reference to bishops, theologians, and exegetes. All have been recognized as teachers of the faith. Avery Dulles has spoken of a dual magisterium. Criticizing Dulles, Ladislas Örsy acknowledges a medieval case for such a view, but along with another theologian, Francis Sullivan, he feels that speaking of a dual magisterium, i.e., bishops and theologians, in our present situation would "lead to endless confusion" and cause misunderstanding. Yet he is clear that the use

16. "Towards a Theology," 151.
17. See "Church Mice," *The Listener* (March 29, 1990).
18. Jude 3.

of the term does not decide the issue, for in fact there has been a *magisterium* of theologians in the church.[19] In certain inter-church contexts *magisterium* has pejorative, even sinister overtones. But the fact remains, theologians have a teaching office in the church. In terms of what our two churches accept as essential oversight, Anglicans and Roman Catholics must acknowledge in their actual praxis the compatibility between the offices of teaching and pastoral care in the person of the bishop.

How we address this situation has implications for the ecclesial relationship of our two communions, for the way we perceive one another, and for the reality of the unity we seek, especially when we speak of freedom, conscience, and obedience.[20] Both teaching offices have responsibilities toward the believing community. Both deserve respect. In a commencement address delivered at the University of Notre Dame on May 18, 1986, James Malone, the Roman Catholic bishop then president of the National Conference of Catholic Bishops, spoke of the balance necessary to ensure co-responsibility toward the Church at large:

> Ultimately theology is a selfless service to the community of believers. The work of theologians receives its definitive meaning when it is integrated with the maturation of the church's faith. It is with this in view that bishops look to theologians and their work for the contributions theologians can make to the people of God.[21]

In a pastoral letter issued by Michael Pfeifer, the Roman Catholic bishop of San Angelo, Texas, in October 1986, we find some evidence of honest concern to get the balance right between the functions of bishop and theologian:

> Throughout Christian history, this interpretation, this guidance whereby the ancient text is applied to the present, has been the work of the bishops. Indeed early bishops, because they were theologians, were often chosen precisely because they had shown an ability to offer this kind of guidance. The unity of the church requires bishops to seek to teach with one voice. . . . Throughout history there have been certain members of the church who have given themselves over to the study of Scripture and of the Christian tradition. . . . These persons assist the church and its official teachers by seeking to offer careful and mature reflection on our faith and its implications. These theologians are also teachers in the faith. . . . In fact, it has often been

19. See Örsy, *The Church,* 63ff.

20. See *Origins,* 16:22 (1986) 391–392.

21. "The Catholic University and the Catholic Community," *Origins* 16:5 (1986) 116–118.

the case that official teaching in the church has been directly based
on the initial study, reflection and teaching of these specialists.[22]

The complementary roles of bishop and theologian are not to be perceived as a system of checks and balances. It is a system of mutual benefits
one to another, in service together for the whole church. The office of
bishop is a more extensive one in that it embraces the function of governing and directly serving efforts toward holiness in the church. This is
reflected in the new Code of Canon Law as already quoted and in the
Decree on the Bishops' Pastoral Office, *Christus Dominus,* of Vatican
II. The following remarks reflect the idiom and thought of Roman Catholics but do not seem out of line with Anglican theology. The function of
the theologian is to assist bishops in the pastoral work of building up a
mature body of Christians for life and witness as the Church in its mission in the world. Faith ever seeks deeper understanding and maturity,
and this is the common task of both bishop and theologian.

Diocesan bishops are local pastors and teachers of the faith. They are
more than administrators or executive officers or symbolic figureheads
of church unity. They are not there to take orders "from above," to be
simply a faithful echo of higher authority. They oversee the whole life
of the whole church in a given place. Bishop Malone expressed this ac-
curately and succinctly: "The local church is not a department of the
universal church, nor is the universal church a federation of local
churches."[23] The service of theologians is mainly one of articulation, speculation, and exploration of the faith in the areas of doctrinal and moral
life. They are expected to teach with a pastoral sensitivity toward people
in their concrete life situations. They have to articulate, speculate, and
explore new frontiers of faith in the world without losing a sense of service to the entire community of faith.

Tensions between bishops and theologians arise particularly when the
theologian speculates and explores and generally opines. The Roman
Catholic Archbishop William Levada feels there would be less tension if
such explorations were not seen as dissent but were "presented as hypothet-
ical, and not as pastoral norms . . . or as substitutes for the accepted

---

22. "Thoughts on Freedom, Conscience and Obedience," *Origins* 16:22 (1986) 391–
392. In this pastoral the United States Catholic Bishops' letters on peace and on the
economy are cited as examples. See also Archbishop William Levada, "Dissent and
the Catholic Religion Teacher," *Origins* 16:10 (1986) 195–199.

23. In his final address on the expiration of his presidency of the National Conference of Catholic Bishops, "The Church: Its Strengths and Its Questions," *Origins* 16:23
(1986) 393–398; See also, "How Bishops and Theologians Relate" in *Origins* 16:9 (1986)
169–174.

understanding of church dogmas.''[24] In summary, if the community of faith, the church, is to live according to the mind of Christ Jesus and extend his mission to the world, bishops need to be nourished by theology. Theologians are more than expert advisors. They are to assist the ministry of *episcopé*. Their articulations, speculations, and explorations are neither irrelevant nor peripheral to the pastoral life and mission of the Church.

Episcopé and Collegiality

Anglicans and Roman Catholics know that the unity they seek will elude them unless they are able to strike a balance between an effective exercise of primacy and an equally effective exercise of conciliarity and collegiality. Both churches must be committed to a future unity without absorption of one by the other. Both want real, visible, credible unity which respects diversity without division. It is therefore of particular interest to both churches to look at the ongoing efforts of the Roman Catholic Church to implement the principles of Vatican II that affect the status and role of bishops as they collaborate in national episcopal conferences.

These episcopal conferences originated in the middle of the last century with the establishment of nation-states, the secularization of society, and the growing socialization of the modern world. They began when the bishops of a particular country initiated such meetings in order to coordinate pastoral practice. Under Pius X and with the promulgation of the 1917 Code of Canon Law, such meetings were encouraged, provided they eschewed a national character and remained purely consultative bodies. These meetings continued and developed into the episcopal conferences we find mentioned in *Christus Dominus* and the apostolic letter of Paul VI entitled *Ecclesiae Sanctae.*[25] The 1983 Code of Canon Law respects this development (Canons 447–459). Pope John XXIII described episcopal conferences as a "privileged instrument of communion and a particularly appropriate organ of episcopal collegiality, practically indispensable in a world in which pastoral action must be measured by a problematic which often exists throughout a nation."[26] These developments are significant

24. "Dissent and the Catholic Religion Teacher," *Origins* 16:10 (1986) 195–199. See also Jon Nilson, "The Rights and Responsibilities of Theologians: A Theological Perspective," *Report of the Canon Law Society and the Catholic Theological Society,* 53–57. Note particularly Nilson's reference to the rights and duties of the theologian toward the hierarchy as "cooperative" rather than "derivative," 61–62. For correspondence on the Vatican's observations of the United States Bishops' text on bishops and theologians, see *Origins* 18:24 (1988) 389–391.

25. *Ecclesiae Sanctae, AAS* 58 (1966) 783–787.

26. Cited from Giorgio Feliciani, "Episcopal Conferences from Vatican II to the 1983 Code of Canon Law," *The Jurist* 48:1 (1989) 11–25. For a review of the develop-

inasmuch as they deepen Roman Catholic renewed understanding of shared oversight or *episcopé*. They encourage Anglican hope that collegiality and a measure of dispersed authority has a place in the Roman Catholic Church. But we must not place an unfair onus on Roman Catholics in efforts to find ways toward full communion. Anglicans must look seriously at the notion of dispersed authority and how it serves the communion of churches. Canon Roger Greenacre's words suggest cautious optimism in this matter. At the end of a critique and response to present tensions over the status and function of episcopal conferences, he says:

> Finally, I have the impression that we are dealing here with two communions which have trajectories going in reverse directions. Both believe in unity in diversity. It seems to me the Roman Catholic Church is at this moment aware of the need to put greater stress on diversity and to find more adequate structures for this; the Anglican Communion finds—at least I hope it does—that it needs at this moment to put a greater stress on unity and to find more adequate structures for it.[27]

Tensions do indeed persist in the Roman Catholic Church over such conferences. In 1988 the Vatican's Congregation for Bishops sent the first draft of a document on the "Theological and Juridical Status of Episcopal Conferences" to each conference of bishops. According to the International Theological Commission, interpreter of *Lumen Gentium* and *Christus Dominus,* "these decrees do not allow one to attribute to episcopal conferences and to a gathering of conferences of a particular continent or area, the quality of collegiality in its full meaning. . . ."[28] This means that such conferences meet the requirements of collegiality only in an analogous sense. The theological reasoning goes this way: Episcopal collegiality is rooted in that of the apostles. As such it refers to the whole episcopate as one body in union with the bishop of Rome. Thus an ecumenical council, and even a synod of all the bishops, fulfills the requirement for authentic collegiality, but an episcopal conference does not. According to the Vatican working paper already referred to, a body such as the National Conference of Catholic Bishops of the United States can exercise only an auxiliary role by enabling diocesan bishops to carry out certain common tasks.[29] These conferences should be described as "col-

---

ment of episcopal conferences, see this work. The entire volume is devoted to the nature and future of such conferences. An Anglican perspective is presented by Canon Roger Greenacre, "Causa Nostra Agitur? An Anglican Response," 384–396.

27. *The Jurist,* 396.

28. See *International Theological Commission: Text and Documents, 1969–1985* (Harrison, N.Y.: Ignatius Press, 1989).

29. See *Origins,* 17:43 (1988) 731–737 for an official Vatican translation of this text.

lective" rather than "collegial," and their function is to deal with practical, pastoral, social issues, not with the formulation and determination of the Church's doctrinal and moral teaching.

In responding to the Vatican's working paper, the bishops of the United States asked for an entirely new approach to episcopal conferences. They seem to have felt that the working paper took into account only one of the several positions that could be derived from the documents of Vatican II. The bishops expressed concern that "without a full presentation of other positions, it might be perceived as lacking objectivity and credibility."[30] Hence the debate has centered on whether the working paper ought to be revised or totally rewritten. While this is an internal debate in the Roman Catholic Church, it has consequences for Anglican–Roman Catholic dialogue. For this reason, it may be helpful to summarize the points of the debate. Underlying both sides of the argument are opinions on the nature and function of *episcopé*. The following schema presents these differences:

Episcopal Conferences: A Summary of the Debate

VATICAN WORKING PAPER

1. Such conferences diminish the teaching role of the diocesan bishop and his proper jurisdiction.

2. They do not possess a mission or mandate to teach doctrine or morals.

3. They bring about the danger of excessive autonomy which makes it impossible to remedy church problems which arise.

4. They create a bureaucracy, often independent of the bishops themselves, made up of "experts" who control bishops.

5. They interfere with the reciprocal relationship between the particular church (diocesan) and the universal church and destroy the equilibrium which is constitutive of the Catholic Church.

6. They are liable to become a divisive occasion for bishops by minority and majority dissent and voting.

CRITICISMS

1. Such conferences are an authentic exercise of collegiality.

---

30. For the official text of the bishops' response, see *Origins* 18:25 (1988) 397–402. Earlier in the year (1988) the president of the United States bishops' conference prepared the way for this response in his address at the National Conference of Catholic Bishops' meeting in Collegeville, Minnesota. For this address see *Origins* 18:8 (1988) 113–117. See also Avery Dulles, "What is the Role of a Bishops' Conference," *Origins* 17:46 (1988) 789–796.

2. To the degree in which they are in communion with the universal episcopate, they exercise a doctrinal function in a truly collegial way.

3. Whether they teach individually or are gathered together in episcopal conferences or particular councils, bishops in communion with the head and the members of the college, while not infallible in their teaching, are the authentic instructors and teachers of the faith for Christ's faithful entrusted to their care (canon 753). It follows that these conferences are pastoral not only in making practical decisions but in teaching the faith as well.

4. The *magisterium,* though unified, exists on different levels, i.e., universal, local, teaching agencies intermediate to universal and diocesan (Dulles).

5. "The *magisterium* is predominantly pastoral in character" (John XXIII). Pastoral is not opposed to doctrinal, i.e., a pastoral *magisterium.*

6. Episcopal conferences cannot impose any belief beyond the general doctrine of the church.

7. Today, especially, bishops cannot teach in isolation.

8. The universal teaching authority of popes and councils cannot adequately meet pastoral needs in every region.

Conclusion

As Anglicans and Roman Catholics pursue their stated goal of seeking full communion, they have to bear in mind that the ultimate goal of ecumenism is the unity of all Christians "that the world may believe." In light of this wider dialogue, which has to deal with questions of authority and oversight in a united church, the New Testament meaning of *episcopé* must be kept at the forefront of the dialogue. There it connotes something of a visitation, an hour of grace which sometimes involves judging (Luke 19:44) and sometimes an exhortation to bear witness as Christians (1 Pet 2:12). Anglicans and Roman Catholics consider *episcopé* to be realized in the teaching office of an ordained person, most particularly in the office of the bishop. Basic to such a person and office is the need to maintain the church as a united community of faith, a living witness to the truth that God has truly visited his people in the person and glorious Gospel of Jesus Christ. Other Christian brothers and sisters in the faith recognize this basic need but do not always associate the requirements of oversight with the single office of the bishop. It may become more understandable to them as they judge its effectiveness by the way it works in our two churches through a more collective or collegial exercise which fully respects the principles of conciliarity and consultation throughout the faithful membership of the church. With our other Christian brothers and sisters, Anglicans and Roman Catholics can continue to build a renewed relationship among all the churches on the model of communion in the New Testament sense of *koinonia*. As *The Final Report* of ARCIC I states, we are not dealing with positions destined to remain static: "Some difficulties will not be wholly resolved until a practical initiative has been taken and our two churches have lived together more visibly in the one *koinonia*."[31] In their various ways this is a suggestion all Christian churches committed to the ecumenical movement can subscribe to here and now.

31. *The Final Report,* "Authority in the Church II," n. 33.

7

Hunthausen

The Bishop and the Bishop of Rome

In 1983 Archbishop Raymond Hunthausen of Seattle was informed by the Holy See that an inquiry was to be made into his administration of the local church. The inquiry was brought on unspecified charges of incompetence and lack of proper doctrinal orthodoxy on the part of the archbishop. Anyone who has been a parish priest knows how difficult it can be at times to toe the line between church doctrine and pastoral practice. That difficulty must be greatly magnified when the bishop of a diocese must make similar decisions. Initially, the Holy See appointed Archbishop James Hickey of Washington, D.C., to assess the situation in the archdiocese of Seattle. Archbishop Hunthausen agreed to this. Ultimately, at the recommendation of Archbishop Hickey, a special commission composed of Archbishops John O'Connor, John Quinn, and Joseph Bernardin was established to address five areas of concern which had been raised by the Holy See: (1) the staffing and adherence to the Code of Canon Law of the Tribunal; (2) the seemingly widespread use of general absolution, First Communion before first confession, and ready acceptance of shared Communion with non-Roman Catholic Christians; (3) the failure to regulate contraceptive sterilizations in Catholic hospitals; (4) ministry to homosexuals; (5) the employment of and liturgical use of non-laicized priests resigned from active ministry, and seminary admission policy and clergy formation.

In his visitation Archbishop Hickey made every effort to assess the credibility of any complaints made to the Holy See by people in the archdiocese of Seattle. Further information was gleaned from what had been made public through the media, from approximately seventy individual interviews, one-third of which were with priests, and from the testimony of Archbishop Hunthausen himself. The investigation revealed that a number of the allegations made against the archbishop were insufficiently based in fact and that the archbishop was already addressing other concerns.

While he was judged competent in many areas, the Holy See "considered him lacking in the firmness necessary to govern an Archdiocese."[1] Consequently, Bishop Donald Wuerl was named as an auxiliary bishop of Seattle whose job was to supervise five areas of ministry in the archdiocese. According to the Holy See, authority in these areas of concern was transferred to Bishop Wuerl for two reasons, to promote the building up of the church in Seattle in harmony with the universal church and to protect the good name of Archbishop Hunthausen.[2] In 1987 Bishop Wuerl was named bishop of Pittsburgh, and full authority was restored to Archbishop Hunthausen.

The series of events in Seattle has unsettled many people. Not only did the incident reinforce Anglican fears, but also for Roman Catholics it raised the question of how the jurisdiction of the local bishop is exercised in relation to that of the bishop of Rome. In speaking for the Roman Catholic bishops of the United States, Bishop James Malone, then president of the National Conference of Catholic Bishops, stated: "The issues raised here touch on the relationship between the local churches and the universal pastor. Bishops exercise their office in communion with him and under his authority."[3] Further, he indicated that the situation in Seattle was beyond the judgmental capacity of the NCCB by Conference stipulation and canon law.

The entire process of the investigation of Seattle was criticized by Archbishop Hunthausen. Mindful not to blame his brother bishops, forthright in his allegiance to the Holy Father, and faithful to the doctrines of the Roman Catholic Church, Hunthausen raised some serious concerns about the process of such an investigation. He criticized the secrecy under which the investigation took place because, he alleged, it compromised the principles of open dialogue within the whole Body of Christ. An open and honestly-aired discussion of events would have been of immense help in alleviating hurt and concern.[4] In September, 1986, Archbishop Francis Hurley of Anchorage indicated a similar concern when he asked:

> "Would an itemization of specifics reveal some fundamental flaws in Archbishop Hunthausen?" Or, he continued, "would they appear trivial and therefore provide feeble basis for the extreme action taken? Only the Holy See can provide the information to resolve that dilemma."[5]

1. *Origins,* 16:23 (1986) 401.
2. *Idem.*
3. *Ibid.,* 400.
4. *Ibid.,* 402.
5. *Origins,* 16:21 (1986) 367.

We might argue here about the efficiency, if not the legitimacy, of the investigation as it took place. On the one hand, "the Holy See's interest in this matter reflected its responsibility for the well being of the universal church as outlined in the Constitution on the Church of the Second Vatican Council."[6] On the other hand, Archbishop Hunthausen himself, speaking to the bishops of the NCCB, voiced his concern that ". . . in many respects the issues of the Seattle visitation are not just issues that touch the life of the Church in Seattle: they are issues that touch the lives of each of our churches in one way or another to a greater or lesser degree." He was also concerned that the apostolic visitation had serious theological implications which "touch very directly and profoundly on our individual role as bishops and on our corporate responsibilities as members of the College of Bishops."[7]

Issues Related to the Case

The Holy See's investigation of the archdiocese of Seattle raises issues unsettling to ecumenical relationships. In ARCIC I's *The Final Report,* the term *episcopé* appears as the touchstone by which all other elements of ecclesial life studied by ARCIC are judged. Furthermore, it seems to be that one of the elements ARCIC found in all the areas of *episcopé* in the church is that of jurisdiction.

In the initial ARCIC I statement on authority, the Venice Statement, the notion of jurisdiction was insufficiently developed. Perhaps the members of the commission assumed that their general treatment of authority in the church could satisfactorily explain jurisdiction without specifically addressing it. This assumption proved to be false. It was left to the Elucidation which followed the Venice Statement and the subsequent ARCIC I Statement (Windsor, paragraphs 16–22) to clarify the matter.[8]

In the Elucidation, ARCIC I defines jurisdiction "as the authority or power (*potestas*) necessary for the effective fulfillment of an office," the exercise and limits of which are determined by that office. It also states that the jurisdiction appropriate to each level of *episcopé* is to "serve and strengthen both the *koinonia* in the community and that between different Christian communities."[9] Furthermore, the jurisdiction granted for the *episcopé* of the church is not always the same but varies according to the level of authority. This definition is repeated in ARCIC's *Authority*

6. *Ibid.,* 362.

7. *Origins,* 16:23 (1986) 401.

8. *The Final Report,* Elucidation (1981), n. 6 and "Authority in the Church II" n. 16–22 (hereafter referred to as *Windsor*).

9. *Ibid.,* n. 6.

of the Church, II (n. 16) in the opening sentences of its treatment of jurisdiction and in its definition of jurisdiction as enjoyed by metropolitans,
bishops, and the universal primate.

> Where a metropolitan has jurisdiction in his province this juris-
> diction is not merely the exercise in a broader context of that exer-
> cised by a bishop in his diocese: it is determined by the specific
> functions which he is required to discharge in relation to his fellow
> bishops.

ARCIC I's Statement on the authority of the bishop of Rome causes
the most anxiety and produces the most discussion. The most pressing
concern on the part of Anglicans is the Roman Catholic attribution of
universal, ordinary, and immediate jurisdiction to the bishop of Rome.
This allows the bishop of Rome to intervene in a diocese anywhere in the
world and to override the authority of the local diocesan bishop in order
to preserve the truth of the faith. ARCIC I explains these terms to those
unfamiliar with them by stating:

> The jurisdiction of the bishop of Rome as universal primate is
> called ordinary and immediate (i.e., not mediated) because it is in-
> herent in his office; it is called universal simply because it must en-
> able him to serve the unity and harmony of the *koinonia* as a whole
> and in each of its parts.[10]

ARCIC I recognized the fears and misgivings of Anglicans. It attempted
to ease them by affirming that the purpose of this jurisdiction is to enable
the universal primate "to further catholicity as well as unity and to foster
and draw together the riches and the diverse traditions of the churches."[11]

An early response from the Roman Catholic Congregation for the Doctrine of the Faith, which was not its last word, was not encouraging. The
Congregation correctly linked ARCIC I's treatment of jurisdiction with paragraph 12 of Windsor where it says that churches out of communion with
Rome have all that is needed, except the papacy, for full union. According to the Congregation, ARCIC I attempted to lessen the Roman Catholic
understanding of what is necessary to allow a Christian body to experience
the full essence of the church. In its opinion, the unity which all the
churches are seeking

> pertains to the intimate structure of faith, permeating all its elements.
> For this reason the office of conserving, fostering and expressing this
> unity in accord with the Lord's will is a constitutive part of the very
> nature of the church (cf. Jn. 21:15-19). The power of jurisdiction over

10. *Windsor,* n. 18.
11. *Windsor,* n. 21.

all the particular churches, therefore, is intrinsic (i.e., *jure divino*) to this office, not something which belongs to it for human reasons nor in order to respond to historical needs.[12]

The common note of contention between CDF and ARCIC I seems to be the formulation of the universal and immediate jurisdiction of the bishop of Rome[13] on which the congregation bases its argument. When Vatican Council I made a pronouncement on this issue, it simply formalized what had been a long-standing doctrine, originally anti-Gallican[14] in purpose but nonetheless offensive to Orthodox, Anglicans, and Old Catholics. In the opinion of some, the theological language of 1870 is out of touch with the contemporary situation, and the definitions of Vatican I might serve the church better if they were restated. Moreover, Vatican Council I did nothing to clarify how the pope could exercise his immediate jurisdiction in a diocese in a way that would strengthen rather than weaken episcopal authority.

The 1988 Anglican Lambeth Conference of Bishops did not initiate new practical measures to hasten the union between Anglicans and Roman Catholics in their response to *The Final Report*. It did commend the work done so far, and acknowledge the "substantial agreement" achieved and encourage further discussions and development.[15]

Conceivably the most important statement in ARCIC I's work on jurisdiction is the following paragraph where the recognized problems and proposed solutions are succinctly presented:

> Although the scope of universal jurisdiction cannot be precisely defined canonically, there are moral limits to its exercise: they derive from the nature of the Church and of the universal primate's pastoral office. By virtue of his jurisdiction, given for the building up of the Church, the universal primate has the right in special cases to

12. "Observations on the Final Report," *Acta Apostolica Sedis* 74 (1982) 1060–1074.

13. "Hence we teach and declare that by appointment of our Lord the Roman Church possesses a superiority of ordinary power over all other Churches, and that this power of jurisdiction of the Roman Pontiff, which is truly episcopal, is immediate; to which all, of whatever rite and dignity, both pastors and faithful, both individually and collectively, are bound by their duty of hierarchical subordination and true obedience, to submit, not only in matters which pertain to faith and morals, but also in those that pertain to the discipline and government of the Church throughout the world, so that the Church of Christ may be one flock under one supreme pastor through the preservation of unity both of communion, and of profession of the same faith with the Roman Pontiff." Denzinger/ Schoenmetzer, *Enchiridion Symbolorum*, 3060.

14. Gallicanism was a seventeenth-century movement in France, the focus of which was to set up a national Catholic Church independent of Rome. Although unsuccessful, its influence was felt for many years.

15. Lambeth Resolutions, 1988, 19–21.

> intervene in the affairs of a diocese and to receive appeals from the decision of a diocesan bishop.[16]

Here the modern principle of subsidiarity must be considered. It states that a higher authority may intervene in a situation only when a lower authority, with ordinary jurisdiction, is unable on its own to maintain the unity of the faith of the Church or adequately respond to matters of discipline. ARCIC I explains this by saying

> It is because the universal primate, in collegial association with his fellow bishops, has the task of safeguarding the faith and the unity of the universal Church that the diocesan bishop is subject to his authority.[17]

Many theologians respond favorably to the statement when it is presented in such a way and situated within the entire framework of the ARCIC I's treatment of jurisdiction. J. Robert Wright, writing in *Ecumenical Trends,* states that there could be general Anglican assent to such an explanation, although the Anglicans would be more ready to use the term *primus inter pares* than universal primate. He notes, however, that this term is usually understood by Anglicans, as it is by Orthodox, "to imply a primacy more of honor than of jurisdiction."[18]

Others have not been so sanguine. Some Anglicans wonder about the value of such a "primacy of honor" and ask, "What is the purpose of honor without authority?" Archbishop Henry McAdoo, a retired bishop of the Church of Ireland and former co-chair of ARCIC I, describes *The Final Report* as not a blueprint for unity but a basis for going forward. A former archbishop of Canterbury, Robert Runcie, welcomed *The Final Report* but "underlined that no one should leap to the conclusion that he or the Anglican General Synod were about to accept the definition of papal jurisdiction."[19] What difficulties there are appear to spring more from the juridical language used than from any theological concern. The Windsor Statement on Authority tries to ease this concern by referring to Pope Paul VI's words spoken at the canonization of the Forty English Martyrs in 1970, when he attempted to reassure Anglicans that reunion with Rome does not mean the suppression of their heritage and traditions.[20] It is only natural that Anglicans should be concerned to guard against the possibility of "laying themselves open to the experience of some of

16. *Windsor,* n. 20.

17. *Idem.*

18. See "ARCIC Final Report: An Anglican Commentary," *Ecumenical Trends* 11 (1982) 152.

19. See "Unity: Not the end, but the beginning," *Universe* (April 12, 1982) 1.

20. *Acta Apostolica Sedis* 62 (1970) 753.

the Uniate Churches which have found their traditions threatened by the Vatican in the interests of canonical uniformity."[21]

Conclusion

The political implications for Anglicans inherent in the jurisdiction of a universal primate in the church must not be forgotten. The English Reformation began with an argument over ecclesiastical jurisdiction in England and this is still an important concern for the Church of England, as it is for all other member Anglican churches throughout the world, each of which is autonomous in its own right. This is not an insoluble problem though. In fact,

> Since most of the interventions of the Pope into the life of Roman Catholic dioceses throughout the world derive from a lower level of jurisdiction than that of universal primate, they presumably need not affect an Anglican Communion not absorbed, but retaining its own canons and customs when united to the Roman See.[22]

Scholars from both faith communities agree that a distinctly Anglican tradition in the church can and must be preserved. It has been pointed out, for example, that paragraph 12 of the Venice Statement states that Vatican I intended to affirm that papal oversight was to be of service to support bishops in the oversight of their dioceses, not to erode that oversight.

Despite these assurances, however, Anglican fears have not been laid to rest. The question of jurisdiction and authority comes immediately to mind, as does collegiality, conciliarity, and *episcopé*. Could the situation in Seattle have been handled better? Was it necessary for the Holy See to intervene directly in local events? Could the NCCB have been utilized to initiate needed reforms and corrections in a more collegial manner? In view of the final outcome and Archbishop Hunthausen's explanation of the areas of concern,[23] does it appear that the Holy See unnecessarily and without proper information intervened in a situation which could have been handled in an entirely different way?

21. Edward J. Yarnold, S.J., "Papal Supremacy and its exercise: Commentary on the final ARCIC report," *Month* 15 (1982) 116.

22. *Catholic Herald* (March 5, 1982) 1. The *Catholic Herald* (Great Britain) further notes: "It is also understood that the ARCIC final report does not necessarily mean the end of the establishment of the Church of England. Anglican members of the commission point out that Papal Concordats with, for example, France are just as restrictive of the choice of bishops by the Holy See as the current powers of the Prime Ministers in episcopal choice in the Church of England."

23. See *Origins* 16:23 (1986) 401–408.

8

Broken Arrow

The Bishop and the Bishop of London

On October 30, 1986, the Right Reverend Graham Leonard, bishop of London in the Church of England, visited and confirmed twenty-one persons at St. Michael's Church in Broken Arrow (Tulsa), Oklahoma. Ordinarily this service—even the presence of a foreign bishop—would have attracted little attention outside the parish. Yet the visit was reported in religious, and some secular, papers in North America and England.

St. Michael's parish had recently severed its ties with the Episcopal Church in the United States (ECUSA), the sister church of the Church of England, and had joined a federation of "continuing Anglican" parishes, loyal to the liturgical traditions of Anglicanism while opposed to developments within the American church which they believe dilute that tradition. Bishop Leonard, a leader of English conservative clergy opposed to such innovations as the ordination of women as priests, acted, moreover, without having obtained the permission of either the Episcopal bishop of Oklahoma, Gerald N. McAllister, or the presiding bishop of the Episcopal Church, Edmond Browning, and despite the express wishes of his own superior, the archbishop of Canterbury, Robert Runcie.

"I made my decision on pastoral care," he insisted after the event. "I have done nothing illegal or uncanonical. . . . I don't think I interfered . . . but I waited until they came out of ECUSA."

This report assesses the official reaction to this historically and theologically unwarranted intrusion by one bishop into the see of another bishop and province of the same communion, and popular reaction, as reflected by the religious press of North America and England to the action.

Episcopal Reception

Knowing the intention of the bishop of London to visit, or to send his suffragan (assistant) bishop to visit, Broken Arrow, the House of

Bishops of the American Episcopal Church protested the proposed visit, citing the history and canons of the American church. By Episcopal Church law, any visiting bishop is obliged to secure the permission of the diocesan bishop before functioning in an episcopal manner within the geographical boundaries of the diocese, whether the ministry is conducted in an Episcopal/Anglican church or in any other religious body.[1] The presiding bishop of the American Episcopal Church had discussed the proposed visit with the archbishop of Canterbury, who had, in turn, requested the bishop of London not to visit or to send his suffragan to confirm members of a church which the American province of the Anglican Communion considered in schism, its priest deposed, and its vestry dismissed.[2] The bishop of London, a priest of the Church of England, which is a member of the Anglican communion of churches to which the Episcopal Church USA also belongs, apparently considered the parish and its priest, which were out of communion with the Episcopal Church, still to be in communion with himself.

The American bishops unanimously approved a motion requesting that any bishop disregarding the canons and disdaining the integrity of a province be challenged and disciplined by the primate and House of Bishops of his own province.

The impropriety of such an action does not depend on the affiliation of the religious body in which the visiting bishop functions:

> Indeed, if a bishop is found to be "exercising episcopal acts in and for a religious body other than this Church . . . without the express consent and commission of the proper authority in this Church," he would be subject to trial and deposition on the grounds of abandoning the communion of this Church.[3]

The collegial nature of the episcopal office, the bishops asserted, demands mutual cooperation and consent:

> It is the expectation of this House of Bishops that the autonomy of the Episcopal Church will be respected by the other branches of the Anglican Communion and all their bishops. It is inappropriate for a bishop in another jurisdiction to assume that he has the authority to judge the competency of our canonical process or to contradict this process. It is equally inappropriate for a bishop to claim the authority which belongs to a province to establish dialogue, enter into communion, or otherwise recognize schismatic groups that style themselves "Episcopal" or "Anglican."

1. Canon 1.13.
2. Journal of the House of Bishops, meeting in San Antonio, September 24, 1986.
3. See Article II, Section 3 of the Constitution, Canon III.15.a(a) and Canon IV.9.

The theological rationale given by the bishops reflects an Anglican understanding of *episcopé*:

> As bishops of the Anglican Communion we are convinced that the episcopal office is not a personal possession. It is the gift of grace recognized by the whole Church to the life of a particular diocese in a particular province. The separation of Holy Orders and their exercise from jurisdiction strikes at the root of catholic faith and polity. Episcopal trust and collegiality are at the heart of our corporate life.

And finally, the bishops viewed as "deplorable, destructive, and irresponsible" the actions of an extra-provincial bishop who would "take under his pastoral and ecclesial care a deposed priest, a dismissed vestry, or a schismatic church," because this action has consequences far beyond the local, or even provincial, level. The arrogation of personal judgment in such a situation, in their view, compromises the order of the entire Church, violates trust and collegiality and destroys the integrity of the decision-making process of every province of the Anglican communion.[4]

The archbishop of Canterbury issued a statement on the day the bishop of London left for Oklahoma, expressing the hope that Dr. Leonard would meet with the bishop of Oklahoma before proceeding, and regretting

> that the Bishop of London, despite the strong objections of myself and of fellow bishops here and in the USA, still thinks it right to exercise sacramental or episcopal care to a congregation which will not accept the discipline of their diocesan bishop.[5]

There is, he reflected later,

> an inherent authority in bishops acting collectively both within and between provinces. A bishop exercises his authority as a member of a college of bishops—symbolized through the laying on of hands of his brother bishops at his consecration. This inherent authority is recognized in our communion—for example, the final decisions about ARCIC have, by the agreement of all the provinces, to be made by the Lambeth Conference [of all Anglican bishops].[6]

The English House of Bishops ruled, after the bishop of London's return from Oklahoma, that a Church of England bishop should not involve himself in the affairs of another province without the consent of

---

4. The above quotations are from the Journal of the House of Bishops, meeting in San Antonio September 25, 1986, with appreciation to the Right Reverend Herbert A. Donovan, Jr., bishop of Arkansas.

5. Reported in *The Church Times,* October 31, 1986.

6. *The Church Times,* November 14, 1986.

the proper authorities.[7] Two English bishops abstained from voting; one opposed the ruling.

The General Synod of the Church of England raised the matter in November, although it was not on their agenda. The archbishop of Canterbury linked the visit to the almost simultaneous unauthorized celebration of the Holy Eucharist by a woman priest visiting London, where the ordination of women was not yet allowed. In both cases, the archbishop reported, he had worked very hard to try to "limit the damage caused in the Anglican Communion." In listing ways open to Anglicans to deal with such a breach of canon and collegiality, he declared that both raised "real issues with which the Communion was already attempting to deal . . . through the Anglican Consultative Council, through meetings of Primates, and through the collegiality of bishops at the Lambeth Conference."[8]

A priest member of the synod questioned the "declared rationale" of the bishop of London and of the woman deacon who had invited the visiting priest to celebrate. In neither case, he believed, were the participants exonerated "in terms of accountability and at least questionable judgment."

> We do not want a witch-hunt, nor do we want to revert to legalism. But how can we consider the meaning of authority in another Church [the ARCIC documents were the subject of the meeting] when the authority in our Church appears to be inoperative, even inoperable.

Another member argued against discussing the cases, which "would open a can of worms which would be better left in the bottom of the boat," and set people to wondering why "the iron hand in the velvet glove had not come down on bishops and others for a variety of other infringements of Church regulations."[9]

The Lambeth Conference of Anglican Bishops 1988

Bishops from all provinces of the Anglican Communion met some two years after the incident, as they do every ten years in pan-Anglican episcopal sessions called Lambeth Conferences (after Lambeth Palace, the London residence of the archbishop of Canterbury). Among the subjects on which declarations were issued by the Twelfth Lambeth Conference, a meeting of 518 bishops at the University of Kent in the summer of 1988, was the ministry and accountability of bishops.

7. *The Church Times,* November 7, 1986.
8. *The Church Times,* November 14, 1986.
9. *Idem.*

While making no direct reference to the incident at Broken Arrow, the bishops at Lambeth issued a strongly worded resolution on the mutual respect which they believed must govern their relationships with one another, not least in a time of transition and disagreement, if they are, as *episkopoi*, to be signs of the unity of the church.

This Conference, they wrote:

> 1. Reaffirms its unity in the historical position of respect for diocesan boundaries and the authority of bishops within these boundaries; and in light of the above,

> 2. Affirms that it is deemed inappropriate behavior for any bishop or priest of this Communion to exercise episcopal or pastoral ministry within another's diocese without first obtaining the permission and invitation of the ecclesial authority thereof.[10]

The Lambeth declaration "Mission and Ministry," moreover, identifies the diocese as basic to the life and unity of the local church and the bishop as the symbol and personification of this unity.[11]

After identifying the bishop as

> a symbol of the Unity of the Church in its mission; a teacher and defender of the faith; a pastor of the pastors and of the laity; an enabler in the preaching of the Word, and in the administration of the sacraments; a leader in mission and an initiator of outreach to the world surrounding the community of the faithful; a shepherd who nurtures and cares for the flock of God; a physician to whom are brought the wounds of society; a voice of conscience within the society in which the local Church is placed; a prophet who proclaims the justice of God in the context of the Gospel of loving redemption; a head of the family in its wholeness, its misery and its joy. . . .[12]

the statement goes on to discuss the collegiality and accountability of Anglican bishops.

Defining the church biblically and as a body and its members as "mutually interdependent," "Mission and Ministry" points to the need for bishops "to work cooperatively within the total Church . . . with the laity, deacons, priests and other bishops (if applicable) of the diocese, with the bishops of other dioceses with whom the bishop is in communion, [and] with other Christian Churches with whom some degree of communion exists." Because each diocese is related to all other dioceses through its bishop, the statement continues,

10. Resolution 72, *The Truth Shall Make You Free,* The Lambeth Conference 1988 (London: The Church House, for the Anglican Consultative Council, 1988) 240.

11. "Mission and Ministry," section 151.

12. "Mission and Ministry," section 152.

We note the need for the bishop and the diocese to be encouraged
to see themselves as mutually accountable to each other for their ministries as well as to the Provinces to which they belong. . . .[13]

No disciplinary measures applicable to a bishop who acts unilaterally,
without consultation with his own metropolitan, with other bishops of
his province, or with bishops of dioceses in other provinces, are mentioned.

The Eames Report

One cause of theological and disciplinary disagreement among Anglicans, and a pastoral concern to the Anglican bishops at Lambeth 1988,
was the ordination of women to the priesthood and (at that point poten-
tially) to the episcopate. This is an extension of sacramental ordination
authorized by some provinces of the church and not by others, and a discipline enthusiastically endorsed by some bishops and intransigently opposed by others.

Immediately following the Conference, in September 1988, an inter-
Anglican commission was appointed, under the chairmanship of the Most
Reverend Robert H. A. Eames, archbishop of Armagh and primate of
the Church of Ireland, to examine the relationships among provinces of
the Anglican communion "and ensure that the process of reception includes continuing consultation with other Churches as well; [and] to monitor and encourage the process of consultation within the Communion and
to offer further pastoral guidelines."[14]

While the subject under discussion was not episcopal visitation but the
collegiality and courtesy of dissenting bishops, several points applicable
to the Broken Arrow incident emerged as the commission discussed how
to maintain "the highest degree of communion" in the face of honest and
heartfelt dissent. "In this process of reception," the report states, in considering bishops in disagreement with the decisions of the House of Bishops
of their own province, "bishops in particular have a special responsibility
to be sensitive both to the mind of the synod and to the collegiality of
the house of bishops. While they may express disagreement with the mind
of their provincial synod, they ought not actively to obstruct that decision."[15]

Laypersons and clergy of various Anglican provinces, the Eames Commission pointed out, are "free to receive the Holy Communion in

13. "Mission and Ministry," section 155.
14. *Report of the Archbishop of Canterbury's Commission on Communion and
Women in the Episcopate 1989* (London: Anglican Consultative Council, 1989) 5. Resolution I, Lambeth Conference 1988 [The Eames Report].
15. The Eames Report, #31, 16–17.

Provinces of different principles and practice; and this as of right rather than by ecumenical hospitality." As the discipline of the Episcopal Church USA ecumenically permits baptized persons who are committed members of their own ecclesiastical body to receive Holy Communion at Episcopal altars, there would be no juridical impediment to a "continuing Anglican" receiving the sacraments at the hand of a priest or bishop of the Anglican Communion. It is, the commission pointed out, "an excessive concentration on the ordained ministry [which] can mislead us into thinking that communion is only to be defined in terms of the interchangeability of ministries."[16]

"Acceptance of anomaly," moreover, is not to Anglicans "the compromise of truth. It is to take seriously the imperative to maintain the unity of the Church."[17] To address the problems posed by the recognition by some Anglican provinces of women in Holy Orders, and the refusal of other provinces to grant this recognition, the Eames Report cites Resolution 72 of the 1988 Lambeth Conference (cited above), repeats and elucidates its definition of the role of the bishop, and admonishes that "where bishops minister in dioceses and/or provinces in which there is strong division of opinion on the ordination of women to the episcopate, they should exercise special care lest they cease to be agents of unity by becoming focal points of dissension."[18]

The report expands this to note that "where visiting bishops accept invitations to exercise the ministry of the Word, they should do so in ways which foster the overall edification of the whole Church."[19] Visiting bishops exercising sacramental ministry, moreover, should "uphold the canonical position of the Province from which they come, out of respect for the local church which they represent," and their episcopal presence "should not become an occasion of divisive demonstration."[20]

Religious Press Reports

The only means of assessing lay reaction to the Broken Arrow incident is provided by the news media. All the news magazines surveyed,[21]

16. The Eames Report, #46, 21.
17. The Eames Report, #53, 23.
18. The Eames Report, #57, 24–25.
19. The Eames Report, #61, 25.
20. The Eames Report, #61, 26.
21. Religious Publications surveyed are:
      The Anglican Digest (ECUSA)
      The Canadian Churchman (Anglican Church of Canada)
      The Christian Challenge (traditionalist Anglicans)

whether Episcopal, Roman Catholic, or other, were at the time reporting on the Curran affair and on the Vatican's treatment of Archbishop Hunthausen, and most apparently did not feel an inter-Anglican tempest on the frontier worth reporting. General religious publications showed no interest whatever in the incident. Only those publications with a marked sympathy for continuing Anglicanism provided details.

The Anglican Digest, a fairly conservative publication of the Episcopal Church, contented itself with linking this incident with that of the unauthorized Eucharistic celebration of an American woman priest in England, remarking that "Authority in the Church was an issue on both sides of the Atlantic this fall. . . ." (Lent 1987, 40).

The Canadian Churchman, the official organ of the Anglican Church of Canada, devoted half a tabloid page in its December 1986 issue to the incident, taking as its point of departure the expressed prior disapproval of the archbishop of Canterbury and, secondarily, the disapproval and objections of the American House of Bishops. It reported, too, that the National Executive Council of the Anglican Church of Canada, a body of fifteen bishops, clergy, and lay persons, had "unanimously approved a resolution registering their dismay over the bishop of London's 'unauthorized involvement' and conveying its support to the House of Bishops in England and the US."

The Living Church, a journal of the Episcopal Church with an editorial policy supporting [Anglican] Catholic doctrine and discipline, reported impassively on events as they unfolded. In their September 26, 1986 issue one-and-a-half columns were devoted to Bishop Leonard's decision to "adopt" the Oklahoma parish, and the diocese of Oklahoma's inability to wrest control of the parish buildings from the "continuing Anglican" congregation of Fr. John Pasco, its pastor. It quotes Bishop Leonard as saying he took the action not as a bishop of the Church of England but as a bishop in "the Church of God," as well as evangelical reaction which equated the statement with " 'mere casuistry' of a kind that Anglicans have traditionally opposed when practiced by the Roman Catholic Church."

Christianity and Crisis
Christianity Today (general Protestant)
The Christian Century (general Protestant)
The Ecumenist
The Episcopalian (ECUSA)
The Living Church (ECUSA)
Origins (RC)

The November 2, 1986 issue contained the full text of the resolution of the House of Bishops of the Episcopal Church without editorial comment. The November 23 issue reported on Bishop Leonard's visit to Oklahoma, noting the disapproval of both American and English Houses of Bishops.

Letters to the editor continued the coverage and raised issues of authority, obedience to canons and tradition, and hopes for equal sensitivity in the matter of the episcopal ordination of women.

The Episcopalian (December 1986), the official Episcopal Church newspaper, devoted two columns to the event, beginning with the disapproval of bishops in both England and the United States, and noting that Bishop Leonard also visited three Episcopal parishes in Philadelphia but cancelled confirmation "and other episcopal" services there upon instructions from the diocesan bishop, Lyman Ogilby. This paper also noted that Bishop Leonard had been assisted at the confirmations at Broken Arrow by retired Episcopal Bishop Clarence Haden.

The Christian Challenge, published by continuing Anglicans, devoted three full pages in its September 1986 issue to printing (and highlighting passages in) correspondence from a position paper by Bishop Leonard about the matter of his relationship to St. Michael's Church, Broken Arrow. In his paper the bishop pointed to the "great difficulty and distress" brought to the consciences of those holding traditional beliefs and ecclesiology by the increasing pernicious "belief in the omnipotence of [provincial] synods and conventions" within the ever more autonomous and nationalistic churches of the Anglican communion, the relativist attitude to Scripture rampant today, abandonment of the Book of Common Prayer and subsequent expression liturgically of changes of doctrine undeliberated by the full church. He decried the diminishment of the role of the historic episcopate brought about by women's ordination—something he felt would become yet graver if women were to be consecrated bishops. In the light of all this, he then articulated the responsibility of "any bishop in the Anglican Communion, who believes that he has the responsibility of being a guardian of the apostolic and traditional faith," to act as "a Bishop of the One Holy Catholic and Apostolic Church, not merely of a particular national Church," and his relationship with "fellow bishops if he believes they have departed from the apostolic ministry." He declared that he would act pastorally, and privately, to anyone asking guidance; he would treat persons outside his own communion, whether formerly within the Anglican Communion or always outside it, on an equal, ecumenical basis. Any bishop in the Anglican Communion is, he believed, not only free but has a duty "to offer the sacraments to Priests and people who have been dispossessed because they wish to remain faithful to traditional Anglican belief [and who] wish, for that very reason to be in communion with a bishop and a bishop who is within the Anglican Communion, [because they do not wish] . . . to become Congregationalists.'' At the same time Bishop Leonard held that ''he should not offer them such communion until they have ceased to be recognized by their original Church within the Anglican Communion''—the situation which obtained at Broken Arrow. ''What the bishop does,'' he concluded, ''is recognize that though expelled, they are orthodox in faith and practice and [that he is] in communion with them.''

The October 1986 issue printed three short articles on Bishop Leonard's visit to Tulsa, criticism in *The Church Times*, and Bishop Leonard's response to it: ''When all is said and done, the fact remains that Father Pasco and his people are no longer in ECUSA. Is no one to care for them?''

The November/December 1986 issue devoted two pages to the brewing storm under the headline ''The London-Oklahoma Link: Lambeth Keeps Quiet; Episcopal Bishops Don't.''

The January/February 1987 issue devoted eight full illustrated pages to the story ''London Comes to Broken Arrow . . . Compassion or Intrusion?'' The author, Dr. Robert Strippy, had attended both the confirmation service and press conferences. He expressed his opinion that ''except for some sideline cheering from members of Continuing Anglican churches and from a smattering of supporters in England and other countries, it appeared that *nobody* wanted the Right Reverend Graham Leonard, Bishop of London, to visit St. Michael's Episcopal Church, Broken Arrow, Oklahoma—except the rector and people of St. Michael's itself.'' He pointed to the enormous personal loyalty of members of the congregation to the rector deposed by the Episcopal diocese, to the siege mentality of the parish resulting from ''Father Pasco's intransigence [which] is matched by Bishop McAllister's,'' and to Bishop Leonard's careful distinction between pastoral care and jurisdiction. The bishop's press conference was attended, he reports, by ''representatives of all the major papers in Oklahoma and Texas . . . along with *The Daily Mail* and *The Daily Telegraph* of London, the BBC, British Independent Television, PBS television in America, and National Public Radio.'' The service itself, he felt, was anticlimactic, although ''the local television stations were obviously enchanted with a form of service that (since Vatican II) has largely fallen into disuse, because they all featured it on their late news broadcasts,'' and were impressed with the ''simply jammed'' church. ''The full house was obviously enthralled,'' he wrote. He ended by wondering in print on the consequences of the act, which—in his metaphor—has opened a crack in a dam that threatens to become full flood.

The same issue also contained a further two pages of ''footnotes'' to the visit: Bishop Leonard's subsequent visit to Lambeth Palace, and the

letter of the [ECUSA] Evangelical and Catholic Mission to Bishop Leonard
assuring him "of its prayer and thankful support for the courageous stand
which you continue to make in England in the cause of the historic faith
and practice of the Church of Christ." It also—very helpfully—surveyed
critical comments from the religious press both in England and the States:
The Church Times (negative), *The Episcopalian* (mildly negative), *The
Living Church* ("recently taking a more modernist [than Anglo-Catholic]
theological position"), *The Diocesan Press Service* (obliquely questioning the validity of the confirmations at Broken Arrow), *The Daily Telegraph* ("the fundamental division is between those who wish to preserve
intact the traditional beliefs and ceremonies of the Anglican Church and
those who, according to their critics, are trying to convert that Church
into a trendy vehicle of secular, humanistic liberalism. . . ."), *The Christian News* (a staunchly traditional Lutheran weekly which espoused the
hope that "all publicity may help to get Episcopalians all over the nation
informed about what has been going on in their church"), *The Religious
News Weekly* of Tulsa (lauding Bishop Leonard as a man of conviction),
The Prayer Society–Rio Grande (deploring the insensitivity of the liberals
to lay souls and concern only for "power and financial and materialistic
holdings"), *The Star* of London (suggesting that bishops who, over the
years, have blessed those conscientiously defying authority are now hoist
in their own petard), and *The Observer* ("He will never be archbishop
now, but that may not stop him having more impact on the Church of
England than any other bishop of his generation"). *The Observer* also
noted Bishop Leonard's All Saints' Day visit to Philadelphia, reporting
that "an expected protest by the women priests . . . did not eventuate
. . . though a number were observed receiving the sacrament."

The March 1987 *The Christian Challenge* continued with several follow-
up items: (1) a two page interview with traditionalist English theologian
Dr. William Oddie railing against women's ordination, defending Bishop
Leonard, and asking "why belong to a Church where one doesn't have
to accept the infallibility of the Pope, if we are forced to accept assumed
infallibility of a General Convention or General Synod?"[22] (2) Bishop
Leonard's open statement to members of the Church of England opposed
to the ordination of women to priesthood and standing ready to separate
from General Synod jurisdiction; (3) settlement terms in the court dis-
pute between St. Michael's Parish and the diocese of Oklahoma.

The Church Times of the Church of England reported the incident
at Broken Arrow from the first rumblings to the final echo, always on
the front page. After the bishop of London returned, an editorial assessed

---

22. Father Oddie subsequently passed from the Church of England to the Church
of Rome and, after the Church of England allowed the ordination of women to the
priesthood in 1994, Bishop Leonard did likewise. He was conditionally reordained
a Roman Catholic priest.

the repercussions on the Church of England and the Anglican Communion. While foreseeing no drastic action taken against the bishop, since no one had "yet suggested what drastic action is legally possible," the editors pointed to what they considered the real question: where this leaves him as a guide in church life.

> For many years his orthodoxy or conservatism has appealed especially to those members of the Church of England identifying themselves as either Catholics or Evangelicals, who have always given their hearts to their own heroes rather than to the official system. Dr. Leonard's disregard of the entreaties of his Primate, of all but two of the English House of Bishops and of an apparently unanimous vote of the American House of Bishops is in this tradition and will therefore win the sympathy of his supporters. But it must be an embarrassment to efforts now being made, in accordance with other Catholic and Evangelical traditions, to discipline other dissentients, such as those who want to invite women priests to officiate in this country.
> Our own view remains that it is not the Anglican way to do more than appeal to the consciences of the dissentients in any matter where the rights of those consciences are pleaded. Such appeals are possible, for not even a morally respectable dissenter is exempt from the obligation to argue a particular case. Over Tulsa we hope that Dr. Leonard will come to see why none of his arguments has so far convinced other bishops, let alone most onlookers. . . .
> Clearly, he has no intention of blessing all such rebels, either in London or elsewhere in the Anglican or ex-Anglican world. Why then has he decided to favor this single, far-off parish. . . .
> The real tragedy of Tulsa is that the Bishop of London has given no sign at all that he really cares about the feelings of those American Anglicans who, disagreeing with him, yet constitute the vast majority—and, judging by the reported comments of the [London suffragan] bishop of Stepney, not enough signs of being careful about the unity of his own diocese. Presumably, he will remain in office; but for most Anglicans, who want unity, respect for his office and respect for his conscience will not be accompanied by respect for his wisdom.[23]

To this, the bishop of London speaking in General Synod, replied:

> We in the Church are deeply affected by this idea that the truth is determined by majority votes . . . but in matters of doctrine, it cannot be. I don't pretend I'm infallible, any more than the General Synod is infallible—but certain people are sometimes called to say, "Stop! Be Careful!"—which is not very popular, but it has to be said.[24]

23. *The Church Times,* November 14, 1986.
24. *The Church Times,* November 7, 1986.

Conclusion

In summary, what light does the melodramatically titled "Incident at Broken Arrow" cast on the question of ecumenical reception? It reveals first, that the intrusion of one bishop into the jurisdiction of another is a matter chiefly of concern to bishops and to those who feel their theological or disciplinary position has been supported. By refraining from comment the Roman Catholic press may charitably have ignored an opportunity to point out that, in comparison to their own disciplinary measures, those available to Anglican prelates are cumbersome and inefficient, or they may simply not have considered the event worth reporting. Private expressions of support to the diocesan bishop, or to the visiting bishop, remain unrecorded.

If the press reports indicate popular reception, then we must conclude that English ecclesiastics, continuing Anglicans, and Episcopalians sympathetic to their defence of traditional Anglicanism followed the events with intense interest. Most Episcopalians were mildly interested. Local interest in the "Bible Belt" was high, but members of other Christian bodies elsewhere felt scarcely a ripple.

Rome, as we see elsewhere in this study, would surely have reacted much differently than did Canterbury, had the incident concerned a dissenting Catholic parish and an overseas bishop. The immediate and universal jurisdiction of the bishop of Rome is written into the Roman Catholic Code of Canon Law. A refusal to concentrate and centralize authority has, however, been a principle of Anglican ecclesiology since the Reformation, and theologians appeal in defense of this stance to the example of the early undivided, but often quarreling, church. Had the interloping bishop been a member of the Episcopal Church, the American House of Bishops would have had the authority to censure and to discipline him. There is, however, no mechanism for discipline between member churches of the Anglican communion. It is a communion, not an ecclesial corporation. As *The Church Times* pointed out: ". . . it is not the Anglican way to do more than appeal to the consciences of dissentients in any matter where the rights of those consciences are pleaded." Anglicans have developed a system of preferring exhortations to charity and collegiality over centralized command.

9

Jenkins

The Bishop as Theologian

On April 29, 1984, David Jenkins, an Anglican theologian, was one of a panel of academics interviewed on British television in a religious program called *Credo*. *Credo* focused on issues of current theological scholarship, bringing together on this occasion a distinguished panel to discuss possible legendary strands in the Gospel story, not least the question of miracles. Jenkins' contribution raised questions about how we should interpret stories of the virgin birth and resurrection of Jesus. His theological stance within the contemporary Church of England is liberal in that he seeks to interpret traditional doctrines in a contemporary manner. Jenkins' declaration on *Credo* became national news because he had just been announced as the bishop-designate of Durham. In the public mind, David Jenkins' pronouncements were no longer those of a university don. They were the words of a bishop, albeit not yet consecrated, about to serve the fourth most senior diocese in the Church of England.

Why did Jenkins' forthcoming elevation to the episcopate make his views a matter of serious debate? Is it permissible for a theologian who is a priest to make a statement which would be inappropriate for a bishop who is a theologian?

The Role of Bishops

A bishop is a guardian of the apostolic faith. Both Roman Catholics and Episcopalians agree on this. As guardian of the faith, the bishop is called to expound as well as defend that faith. Characteristically this involves preaching. It also means writing articles, especially in diocesan publications. Sometimes the bishop is called upon to lecture on matters of faith and doctrine. Some bishops even assume responsibility for writing learned articles and books.

In proclaiming the apostolic faith, the bishop has to ask: how do I proclaim this faith in the modern world? Take, for example, the doctrine of the Trinity. What are legitimate and what are illegitimate explanations of this mystery? Clearly, it is not enough merely to state the doctrine that God is both three and one.

The doctrine of the Trinity has to be accepted by the faithful. It therefore needs to be explained in thought forms and expressions that are both consonant with the apostolic faith and comprehensible to contemporary people. Since the thirteenth century, bishops have looked to theologians for help with this task. Both theologians and bishops are called to uphold the apostolic faith. Their roles are complementary, but their emphasis and their audiences differ. Because the bishop's task is to guard the faith, he tends naturally to focus on the preservation of long-established doctrinal truth. The theologian's role is more experimental, often asking how established doctrine can best be presented in the modern world. In an ideal world—and an ideal Church—the bishops and theologians would be in perfect accord. In a real world, and in the real Church, there are instances where bishop and theologian disagree, with the bishop stressing fidelity to the tradition and the theologian emphasizing a need to recast or reformulate a doctrine.

A series of questions arises when the bishop is himself a theologian. To what extent does the bishop, as guardian of the faith, have the theologian's right to explore new ways of expressing the faith? Should a bishop who is also a theologian publicly express doubts over traditional ways of expressing Christian doctrine? To put it another way: what constraints must a theologian place upon himself when he accepts a call to the episcopate? Furthermore, what legitimate constraints should be placed upon a bishop's personal theological utterances—and by whom?

The Jenkins Affair

This question lies at the heart of a controversy raised by the election of David Jenkins as bishop of Durham. Durham has a distinguished tradition of scholar bishops who have made a significant impact upon the Church of England. Therefore, when David Jenkins' appointment was announced on March 14, 1984, the news caused little stir. He was known as a gifted theologian, well grounded in the historic faith, yet willing to pursue new avenues of thought.

Few, if any, predicted the impact he would make so soon upon the ordinary believer, via the media. Whether commenting on a coal miners' strike or discussing the nature of miracle, David Jenkins captured the headlines. Two incidents brought Jenkins' name to the forefront of common theological debate in Britain. The first, the television interview already mentioned, took place before Jenkins' consecration as a bishop. In this discussion of the plausibility of miracles, Jenkins enraged many traditionalist Anglicans by his failure to interpret literally the church's teaching first on the virginal conception of Jesus and, second, on his resurrection.

The second incident took place three days after Jenkins' consecration on July 6, 1984, at York Minster, the seat of the archbishop of York, primate of the province to which Durham belongs. At 2:30 a.m. on July 9, the Minster caught fire. Ted Harrison has described the scene:

> The ancient timbers at the southern end of the south transept roof had caught alight. Firemen described the burning building as being like a huge Roman candle; flames and sparks were soaring to the top of the two-hundred-foot tower. As the inferno raged, the oak vaulting—the product of years of faithful craftsmanship and recent restoration—smouldered, charred and turned to charcoal and ash. The glass in the irreplaceable windows cracked and the lead buckled and melted with the heat.[1]

Some who deemed Jenkins' remarks a clear repudiation of essential Christian doctrines asked whether God had caused lightning to strike. Could it be a sign of divine displeasure at the heretical views of one who had so recently been consecrated at York Minster?

We need to ask why Jenkins' views had such an impact in Britain. It was simply because they were the utterances of a bishop-designate. Especially to the more conservative faithful of Britain, a senior bishop was undermining the faith which he should be guarding. Theologians and bishops who share Jenkins' views invariably air them in scholarly tomes, unread by the great bulk of churchgoers, lay or ordained. Jenkins had expressed them on television, making headline news. His theological opinions sold copy. For that reason alone they had to be dealt with.

What Jenkins Said

What did Jenkins actually say? Ted Harrison has preserved a transcript of the original *Credo* interview in *The Durham Phenomenon*. We must remember that these were "off-the-cuff" remarks, not as clearly and logically expressed as Jenkins' theological writings. Neither can we relive

---

1. Ted Harrison, *The Durham Phenomenon* (London: Darton, Longman and Todd, 1985) 1. Harrison's book is a major source for the events and views described in this chapter. For a first-hand account of the events, see David Jenkins and Rebecca Jenkins, *Free to Believe* (London: BBC Books, 1991). The *Preface* reveals that the book was composed by Rebecca Jenkins but "the outline . . . the arguments of each chapter and the draft of every page has been discussed again and again between the

the gestures nor the give-and-take of a television interview. Phillip White-head, the interviewer, posed the following question to David Jenkins:

> Professor Jenkins, do churchmen like you hold the view that mi-raculous details of the story of Jesus, like his birth to a virgin or the fact that he walked on the water, ought to be taken as representing the literal truth today?
>
> David Jenkins: No, but I think it is important to make some dis-tinctions. There's a distinction, it seems to me, between miracles which are events which seem to happen when people are getting excited about important matters and which raise wonder, so I think it quite likely that Jesus performed miracles or was thought to perform miracles. And then there's the question of telling miraculous stories because you've already had a wonderful belief, and I think the virgin birth is like that—I mean, to show people really believed that he came from God and all the rest of it, they told the story of the virgin birth. And then there's finally the resurrection which I think is a whole different kettle of fish, but I expect you'll come to that.[2]

Jenkins' remarks have an informal, conversational and even loose tone to them. They are not the guarded words of theological debate. (Profes-sional theologians are unlikely to allude to the resurrection as "a whole different kettle of fish.") But however informal, David Jenkins' words were those of the bishop-elect of Durham, and they seemed to question whether the virgin birth was an actual historic event. He continued:

> The virgin birth, I'm pretty clear is a story told after the event in order to express and symbolize a faith that this Jesus was a unique event from God, you see, so it's different from the other miracles in my view, and I mean, if I might be allowed to say so, I wouldn't put it past God to arrange a virgin birth if he wanted but I very much doubt if he would, because it seems contrary to the way in which he deals with persons and brings his wonders out of natural personal rela-tionships.[3]

Shortly thereafter the interviewer asked Jenkins in effect whether the infancy narratives were grounded in historical fact or were they rather a series of stories which had been constructed in retrospect in order to accent the uniqueness of Jesus? Jenkins replied: "Yes, and the belief al-ready held, that is what I . . . yes, I think so."[4]

---

two authors" so that "the resulting book presents and represents David Jenkins' thoughts." Another helpful discussion of the issues involved is the Modern Church-men's Union Pamphlet 15 in the *Forewords* series by David Edwards and titled *Bishops and Beliefs*. The pamphlet is undated.

2. *Ibid.*, 19–20.
3. *Ibid.*, 20–21.
4. *Ibid.*, 21.

The conversation turned to the resurrection. "Do you hold the view," asked Phillip Whitehead, "that Jesus rose from the dead and ascended into heaven?" Jenkins responded:

> Well, I hold the view that he rose from the dead. The question is what that means, isn't it? . . . [I]t doesn't seem to me, reading the records as they remain in both the Gospels and what Paul says in 1 Corinthians, that there was any one event which you could identify with the resurrection. What seems to me to have happened is that there were a series of experiences which convinced, gradually convinced, a growing number of the people who became apostles that Jesus had certainly been dead, certainly buried and he wasn't finished, and what is more he wasn't just not finished but he was raised up, that is to say, the very life and power and purpose and personality which was in him was actually continuing, and was continuing both in the sphere of God and in the sphere of history, so that he was a risen and living presence and possibility.[5]

Jenkins went on to affirm that the experience of the risen Christ was an objective encounter with God, not merely a phantasm of the imagination.

Jenkins' opinion that there was no one specific action which constituted the resurrection caused consternation. In particular it left unanswered questions about whether he believed that the tomb of Jesus had been found empty on that first Easter Day and whether the empty tomb was objective evidence of Jesus' physical resurrection. Jenkins' critics saw his words as disturbing signs of a theologically liberal stance on the resurrection and the virgin birth. To them, both the resurrection and the virgin birth were historically verifiable events—in short, the tomb was empty and Jesus of Nazareth had been born of a virgin.

Within a month of the television interview, Jenkins explained his stance on the resurrection during a BBC Radio 4 religious program, *Sunday*. Jenkins said: "Supposing the tomb was empty, and it may have been, that is not the resurrection. The resurrection is being sure of the Living Lord."[6] In the case of the virgin birth, Jenkins was distinguishing the historical question of whether Jesus was born of a virgin from the doctrine of the Incarnation which is the belief that God became fully human in Jesus of Nazareth. Likewise Jenkins insisted that belief in the resurrection—that God raised Jesus from the dead and that he is alive in the Godhead—is not dependent on historically proving that his tomb is empty.

5. *Ibid.,* 21–22.
6. *Ibid.,* 51.

General Reactions

Initial reaction to David Jenkins' remarks on *Credo* indicated that within English society an Anglican bishop is clearly seen as the guardian of the faith. The Reverend William Ledwich, chaplain of Hereford Cathedral School, immediately drew up a petition asking the archbishop of York, the Right Reverend Dr. John Habgood, not to consecrate David Jenkins. More than twelve thousand communicants had added their signature when on July 1, five days before the date set for the consecration, Mr. Ledwich, accompanied by others, presented his petition to the archbishop.

The Jenkins' case was again news. The *Church Times* was bombarded with correspondence. An editorial in the evangelical *Church of England Newspaper* described Jenkins as "a hindrance rather than a help to the people of God" and accused him of taking "pride in peddling dangerous and foolish heresy."[7] Some conservative or traditional Anglicans set up a new organization called Action for Biblical Witness to Our Nation. On June 22, eleven clerical members of the Convocation of York (the synod) sent a letter to the archbishop of York asking that David Jenkins' views be discussed by the General Synod itself before his consecration.

On Sunday, June 24, *Credo,* the television program on which Jenkins had originally broadcast his controversial interview, announced that it had polled thirty-one of the thirty-nine English diocesan bishops. Eighteen bishops, it was claimed, held a traditional view of the virgin birth, ten thought it was a story added after the event, and three kept an open mind on it. On the resurrection, twenty bishops believed that Jesus had come back from the dead, either physically or as a spirit in human form, two claimed open minds and nine bishops thought that the story of the resurrection "arose from a series of experiences that convinced Jesus' followers that he was alive among them after his death."[8]

To what extent did the archbishop of York hear and respond to the petitions and concerns brought before him? Three days after receiving Mr. Ledwich's petition and two days before the consecration, Dr. Habgood issued his response, referring to two Church of England reports. In 1938, the Church of England's Report on Doctrine had

> recognized that the Creeds contain many types of statement in which
> the borderline between the symbolic and the historical dimensions can-
> not be precisely defined, and it explicitly affirmed a liberty of interpre-

7. *Ibid.,* 50.

8. *Church Times,* June 29, 1984. The *Daily Telegraph* carried an article on Jenkins on July 8, 1984, in which the writer, Sebastian Faulks, commented thus on the two bishops who were not prepared to commit themselves on the resurrection: "Their Easter services must be interesting. 'We are here today to celebrate the victory of Christ over death. Probably. Please kneel. Or sit.'"

tation . . . [Although] such liberty must not be taken so far as to undermine the historical basis of the gospel itself.

The 1981 Doctrine Report, *Believing in the Church,* assumed a similar liberty of interpretation.[9]

The archbishop added that at the consecration service David Jenkins would have to affirm his belief in the doctrine of the Christian faith as the Church of England has received it. Any charge that David Jenkins could not appropriately make this vow "would need to be backed by evidence from his writings and other well-considered expressions of his belief." Archbishop Habgood questioned "whether a bishop's orthodoxy should be judged by his writings, the general tenor of his teaching and his formal profession of faith, or by brief, unscripted and epigrammatic remarks made to the media?" He then implicitly recognized the need for a bishop who is also a creative and speculative theologian to distinguish those roles when speaking publicly. Dr. Habgood conceded that it could be argued that David Jenkins had been:

unwise in the manner he has expressed himself publicly. No doubt he will quickly learn that the way a bishop is heard differs from the way a professor is heard.

Dr. Habgood then consecrated David Jenkins on the date originally set.

The Response of the Bishops

The debate engendered by Jenkins' views did not go away. Questions were asked in the General Synod of the Church of England on February 13, 1985, about the House of Bishops' corporate affirmation of the teaching of the Church of England. The bishops responded in a report entitled, *The Nature of Christian Belief,* dated April 1986.[10] The House of Bishops' decision to act corporately is fully consistent with this judgment from the ARCIC I statement of 1976 which states that "bishops are collectively responsible for defending and interpreting the apostolic faith."[11]

In *The Nature of Christian Belief* the House of Bishops unequivocally affirmed their adherence to their church's faith:

[W]e are united in our adherence to the apostolic faith which the Church of England has received and in which it lives. That faith is

9. For the complete text of Archbishop Habgood's remarks see *Church Times,* July 6, 1984.

10. *The Nature of Christian Belief: A Statement and Exposition by the House of Bishops of the General Synod of the Church of England* (London: Church House Publishing, 1986).

11. *The Final Report,* 63.

uniquely revealed in the Holy Scriptures, and set forth in the catholic Creeds, and to it the official formularies of the Church of England bear witness.[12]

More specifically, the House of Bishops' report affirms the Church of England's belief in the objective reality of the resurrection of Christ, the historical veracity of the story of Christ's empty tomb, the divinity of Christ, and his virginal conception. The relevant passages in the report are as follows:

> (2) We affirm our faith in the Resurrection of Our Lord Jesus Christ as an objective reality, both historical and divine, not as a way of speaking about the faith of his followers, but as a fact on which their testimony depends for its truth.
>
> (3) As regards belief that Christ's tomb was empty on the first Easter Day, we acknowledge and uphold this as expressing the faith of the Church of England, and as affirming that in the resurrection life the material order is redeemed, and the fulness of human nature, bodily, mental and spiritual, is glorified for eternity.
>
> (4) We declare our faith in the affirmation of the catholic Creeds that in Jesus Christ, fully God and fully human, the Second person of the Blessed Trinity is incarnate.
>
> (5) As regards the Virginal Conception of Our Lord, we acknowledge and uphold belief in this as expressing the faith of the Church of England, and as affirming that in Christ God has taken the initiative for our salvation by uniting with himself our human nature, so bringing to birth a new humanity.[13]

Not everything in *The Nature of Belief* satisfied Bishop Jenkins' conservative opponents. They would have preferred a stronger affirmation of what they considered the undoubted and objective reality of the empty tomb and the virginal conception of Christ than the phrase "expressing the faith of the Church of England" might be taken to imply.

Clearly the House of Bishops of the Church of England saw it as their role to pronounce on central matters of the church's faith in the light of questions initiated by the controversy over David Jenkins. Episcopal oversight involves guardianship of the apostolic faith. This is written into the Constitution of the General Synod of the Church of England. Indeed, Article 7 states:

> A provision touching doctrinal formulae of the services or ceremonies of the Church of England or the administration of the Sacraments or sacred rites thereof shall, before it is finally approved by the Synod, be referred to the House of Bishops, and shall be submit-

12. *The Nature of Christian Belief,* 1.
13. *Ibid.,* 2.

ted for such final approval in terms proposed by the House of Bishops
and not otherwise.[14]

The constitution of the General Synod of the Church of England places
ultimate responsibility for matters of doctrine upon the House of Bishops.
The bishops themselves, should they desire or need advice, have recourse
to the Doctrine Commission of the Church of England. This has a dual
function. First, it is to consider and advise the House of Bishops upon
doctrinal questions referred to it by the bishops. Second, the Doctrine
Commission is to make suggestions to the House of Bishops as to what
in the commission's judgment are doctrinal issues of concern to the Church
of England. There is a mutuality to the relationship, although final responsibility for pronouncements on doctrine rests with the House of
Bishops.

The preparation and publication of *The Nature of Christian Belief* is
an expression of the *koinonia* in which the episcopate participates. The
report indicates that the House of Bishops envisages its role as much more
than supervisory responsibility in legislating on matters of faith and order.
Rather when the Church is engaged in controversy over the meaning of
the faith, the episcopate of the Church of England interprets its role of
guardianship as demanding active theological commentary.

In responding to David Jenkins' remarks on miracles, the virginal conception of Jesus, and his resurrection, the Church of England found itself
grappling, at the most practical level, with what it means for a bishop
to be both guardian of the faith and a creative theologian. The House
of Bishops' report conceded the tension between guarding, expounding,
and teaching the faith as it has been received, and the complementary role
of being "apostolic pioneers."[15] They maintained that a bishop cannot
be concerned solely with "checking erosion of the fundamentals of
faith."[16] The bishop must also defend the legitimate variety and breadth
of Christian teaching. On the one hand, the report appears to recognize
the danger of fossilizing the church's tradition in the thought forms of

14. The Constitution of the General Synod of the Church of England is reprinted
annually in *The Church of England Year Book* and published in London by the Church
Information Office.

15. *The Nature of Christian Belief,* 35. For a response from David Jenkins himself, see David E. Jenkins, *God, Miracle and the Church of England* (London: SCM
Press, 1987). The first chapter is titled "The Nature of Christian Belief." Jenkins comments in his introduction; "The first [chapter] is my speech to the General Synod of
York on Sunday, July 6, 1986. This was a contribution to the debate on the Report
of the House of Bishops entitled *The Nature of Christian Belief.* The report arose out
of a debate in General Synod in February 1985, which itself rose out of the controver-
sies which I, to some extent, had occasioned" (ix-x).

16. *Ibid.,* 37.

the early centuries of Christendom. On the other hand, an individual bishop, fallen prey to the latest theological fad, cannot speak for the community of the faithful. The report therefore confirms that bishops must be sensitive both to the church's long standing exposition of the faith and to fresh insights. In what could well be taken as a reference to the Jenkins' affair, the report confirms that bishops

> need to distinguish in their own teaching between the well-established fruits of scholarship and those more speculative and controversial hypotheses which have not yet been tested or found acceptance either in the scholarly community as a whole or within the Church.[17]

Thus the bishop needs to make it clear when he is speaking specifically as guardian of the church's faith and when he is engaged as a private theologian.

The last word on the Jenkins' affair came from the General Synod— an indication of the role of all orders in receiving the Church's doctrine. In May 1986, Mrs. Margaret Brown introduced a Private Members Motion to the General Synod. The motion raised the very issues which Jenkins had addressed. It read that

> this Synod affirms that Jesus Christ, the Son of God, was miraculously conceived, through no human fatherhood, in a virgin mother, and that after his crucifixion His dead body which had been laid in the tomb was raised to life by the power of God and revealed in glory to his disciples.[18]

The motion was not discussed until February 19, 1990, when Mrs. Brown had this to say by way of introduction:

> I have brought this motion before the Synod today because I, and thousands of other Christian people, are deeply concerned that there are bishops and clergy in the Church of England who no longer believe in the Virgin Birth and the Bodily Resurrection of Our Lord. If we take out the Virgin Birth and the Bodily Resurrection, we have no Christian religion. I am deeply concerned for the ordinary man and woman in the pew whose faith has been badly shaken by statements of Church leaders that they do not believe in these things.

Various views were brought forth during the debate, not all of them critical of the position held by Bishop Jenkins. Mrs. Jean Mayland, a synod member from York, supported an open approach to Christian doctrine,

---

17. *Ibid.*, 36.

18. This and the following quotations come from the *General Synod Digest*, 14. This is published by Chansitor Publications, Ltd., St. Mary's Plain, Norwich, Norfolk, NR3 3BH, United Kingdom. Pages are unnumbered.

asserting that Anglican truth and belief stressed the incarnation of Jesus and his resurrection, not just the virgin birth and the bodily resurrection. When the debate continued on February 22, its last day, Archbishop Habgood described Mrs. Brown's motion as "unscriptual and untraditional in spelling out in a rather crass way what Scripture spells out in a very subtle way."

By contrast, the Reverend Tony Higton proposed as an amendment "that only those who uphold this traditional belief, including the virginal conception and bodily resurrection of Christ, should be eligible for or remain in episcopal or any other teaching office of the Church." This amendment was overwhelmingly defeated.

A final amendment won the day. This read:

> That this Synod reaffirms the traditional belief about the birth, death and resurrection of Our Lord Jesus Christ as found in the canonical Scriptures and in the Apostles and Nicene Creeds, and to which the Church of England bears witness.

Conclusion

The Jenkins' affair indicates the sensitive role of a bishop in the Church of England when he is also a speculative theologian. It indicates that the bishop has a special responsibility in upholding or guarding the apostolic faith. He should take special care when, like Jenkins, he is also a gifted theologian. The Jenkins' debate also reveals the role played by all members of the laity—whether ordained or not—through the debates of the General Synod. Anglican bishops play the major role in safeguarding the church's faith, especially in matters which touch on matters of liturgical or sacramental order. The clear interplay of all orders within the Church of England in determining the church's faith is consistent with what has come to be referred to among Anglicans as "dispersed authority."

This term derives from a committee report presented by sixty-four bishops at the 1948 Lambeth Conference. Under the section heading "The Meaning and Unity of the Anglican Communion," the bishops included this comment upon authority in Anglicanism:

> Authority, as inherited by the Anglican Communion from the undivided Church of the early centuries of the Christian era, is single in that it is derived from a single Divine source, and reflects within itself the richness and historicity of the divine Revelation, the authority of the eternal Father, the incarnate Son, and the life-giving Spirit. It is distributed among Scripture, Tradition, Creeds, the Ministry of the Word and Sacraments, the witness of saints, and the *consensus fidelium*, which is the continuing experience of the Holy Spirit through

His faithful people in the Church. It is thus a dispersed rather than
a centralized authority having many elements which combine, interact with, and check each other; these elements together contributing
by a process of mutual support, mutual checking, and redressing of
errors or exaggerations to the many-sided fullness of the authority
which Christ has committed to His Church (emphasis added).[19]

Anglican bishops have a clear teaching office. In the Jenkins' case the
report of the House of Bishops, *The Nature of Christian Belief,* was their
appropriate response to doctrinal concerns raised in the Church of England. The bishops take final responsibility for determining what is a legitimate development of doctrine. At the same time, they interact with the
Doctrine Commission, which both informs the House of Bishops of theological issues which may need to be addressed and gives theological coun-
sel to the House of Bishops when required. The rest of the church can
make their views heard through a representative General Synod: in this
instance through Mrs. Brown's private motion. Thus, as in our example,
Anglican bishops have a clear teaching office. In a dispersed authority,
however, the individual utterances of bishops are subject to a variety of
checks and balances as the church either receives or does not receive a
particular teaching as consistent with its own life and faith.

19. *Lambeth Conference 1948* (London: S.P.C.K., 1948) 84–85.

10

Curran

The Bishop and the Theologian

Teaching authority in the Church is a lively and timely topic within the Roman Catholic and Episcopal Churches as well as the secular media. The Curran affair, the June 1990 Vatican statement on theological dissent, and in the more distant past the firestorm following Pope Paul VI's statement in *Humanae Vitae* on the immorality of contraception—all of these events relate directly to the issues of theological dissent and the teaching authority of the *magisterium*.

At issue is whether there exists in the church an authority that can set down normative doctrine on matters of faith and morals, whether all members of the church have an obligation to accept this teaching even if those members have theological objections to accepting it, and whether ministers and theologians of the church are obligated to express publicly only the teachings of the church.

Magisterium and dissent are issues that are directly related to questions of papal authority, episcopal authority, the teaching authority of the college of bishops, and the authority of theologians. It is not surprising that this issue has often been considered in the dialogues and statements of Anglicans and Roman Catholics. Teaching authority has been a topic of dialogue at the international level in the Venice Report of 1976, and its subsequent elucidation and development appear in the ARCIC *The Final Report* of 1981.[1] This topic was of major concern at the national level to ARC–USA in the early 1970s.

Theological Foundations

That the Church of England and the continental Reformation churches have not developed a detailed theology of *magisterium*, dissent, and

1. "Authority in the Church I (Venice 1976)" and "Authority in the Church II (Windsor 1981)," both contained in *The Final Report,* 49–102.

authority is not surprising. Anglicans and Protestants in the sixteenth century were anxious to rid themselves of what they saw as the heavy-handed and excessive authority traditionally associated with the bishop of Rome. By contrast, the Roman Church after the Reformation held even more firmly to a theology of the indefectibility of the church and further developed its traditional teaching of the special role of bishops and pope in guarding and teaching the apostolic doctrine handed down in the church.

The foundation of the contemporary Roman Catholic understanding of dissent and *magisterium* is contained in Vatican Council II's Constitution on Divine Revelation. A key passage for our issue is:

> The task of authentically interpreting the Word of God, whether written or handed on, has been entrusted exclusively to the living teaching office of the Church, whose authority is exercised in the name of Jesus Christ. This teaching office is not above the Word of God, but serves it, teaching only what has been handed on, listening to it devoutly, guarding it scrupulously, and explaining it faithfully by divine commission and with the help of the Holy Spirit; it draws from this only one deposit of faith everything which it presents for belief as divinely revealed.[2]

Yet Vatican II made it clear that this teaching authority is not to be exercised in an isolated manner. The *magisterium* is bound by the *sensus fidei* of the church of this and previous times, and it is also bound by the documents of the tradition in which the common faith of the People of God has been set forth. *Sensus fidei* here means the insight into truth that is possessed by the Christian people as a whole.

Greater detail concerning the relationship between theologians and magisterium within the context of the documents of Vatican II was provided on April 15, 1979, in the Apostolic Constitution *Sapientia Christiana* of Pope John Paul II. This document provided new guidelines for ecclesiastical universities and their faculties in relation to the teaching authority of the *magisterium*. Citing Vatican II's *Lumen Gentium* and *Dei Verbum* as the basis of its teaching, *Sapientia Christiana* argued that academic freedom in "ecclesiastical universities" has a particular meaning:

> True freedom in teaching is necessarily contained within the limits of God's Word, as this is constantly taught by the Church's magisterium . . . true freedom in research is necessarily based upon firm adherence to God's Word and deference to the Church's Magisterium, whose duty it is to interpret authentically the Word of God.[3]

2. *Dei Verbum,* n. 10.

3. *Acta Apostolicae Sedis* 71:7 (May 15, 1979) article 39. See also Jon Nilson, "Bad Law Makes Hard Cases: A Study of the Curran Case," ARC–USA Papers (1989).

Signs of Division

Among events related to dissent and authority, the case of Professor Charles Curran of The Catholic University of America has been notable for the wide discussion it has stimulated on the issue of academic freedom within Roman Catholic institutions. In the summer of 1986 Charles Curran was judged by the Vatican Congregation for the Doctrine of the Faith to be in open dissent from the teaching of the Roman Catholic Church. In the spring of 1987 Professor Curran's classes in theology were canceled at The Catholic University of America, and his tenure to teach theology at the University was revoked. Curran eventually left that university and accepted a number of visiting professorships before moving permanently to an endowed chair at Southern Methodist University in Dallas. The Curran case has defined and publicized honest theological differences that persist between Anglicans and Roman Catholics regarding the right of the Vatican to intervene in the affairs of a national church.[4]

Throughout the nine years of its dealings with Charles Curran, the Vatican had a single aim, to follow its investigatory procedures and to decide whether or not Charles Curran had dissented from the *magisterium's* teaching. For the Vatican Congregation of the Doctrine of the Faith which handled this investigation, *Sapientia Christiana* provided the norms which were to govern Curran's professional activity. Curran frankly admitted that he dissented from some Vatican positions. The Vatican completed its procedures previously outlined in its guidelines and forced Curran out of his teaching position.

What the Vatican cannot have expected was how sharp would be the reaction of Roman Catholic theologians, particularly in the United States, to its resolution of the complicated issues surrounding the relationship between outside authority and free intellectual exploration. On one side were the supporters of the Vatican's intervention, who pointed to "higher values" which override the standards of the American professoriate and applauded those who had the courage to enforce them. Six hundred members of the Fellowship of Catholic Scholars noted that "it is inconceivable that a school at any stage of education can call itself Catholic without simultaneously relating itself to the *magisterium* of the church."[5] The president of The Catholic University of America has stated that a decision of his board of trustees to remove the commission of a professor is consistent with institutional autonomy and not intrusive on academic freedom as long as the Church is acknowledged to have a right to decide who may or may not teach in its name.[6]

4. See R. W. Franklin, "Lessons from the Past Illuminate Curran Affair," *College Teaching* 35:2 (Spring 1987) 50.

5. *Idem.*

6. See William J. Byron, "Credentialed, Commissioned and Free," *America* (August 23, 1986) 69–71.

On the other side were the Catholic Theological Society of America, the College Theology Society, and scores of European Roman Catholic theologians, who called the Curran case and similar developments in Europe a serious challenge to the open and renewed spirit of Vatican II. These groups have pointed to the devastating history of the exercise of power by outside agencies in the sensitive areas of hiring and termination of tenure, to the relationship between effective teaching and research in a Christian university, and to the necessity of autonomy in the face of authority of every kind, lay or clerical, external to the academic community.[7]

The Vatican Response

Partly as a response to this division of opinion, the Congregation for the Doctrine of the Faith issued an "Instruction on the Ecclesial Vocation of the Theologian"[8] in June 1990. This document reflected a heightened concern to limit and contain dissent, a term the congregation uses in a pejorative sense to mean public opposition to the teaching authority of the church. Theologians, the CDF declared, should refrain from giving "untimely public expression" to their divergent opinions, and they should avoid turning to the mass media and seeking to mobilize public opinion to bring pressure on ecclesiastical authorities. The instruction warns against theories of academic freedom that fail to take account of the special character of the theological disciplines, and against the ideology of liberalism. The instruction does not seem to forbid discreet criticism in scholarly journals and theological conferences.

Almost immediately, a group of theologians including Hans Küng and Edward Schillebeeckx published a highly critical response to the Vatican's instruction on the place of the theologian. Our purpose here is not to document Roman Catholic division on this but to demonstrate that the line of papal policy expressed in these documents has been largely rejected by Episcopalians in the United States. In other words, this development concerning dissent and *magisterium* not only has not been "received" by the Episcopal Church, it is creating a new barrier to union. Here we have a case of non-reception and an example that shows that new developments may slow the pace to reconciliation.

The Episcopal Response

To show how this development has slowed the pace of ecumenism we turn to the example of the seminaries of the Episcopal Church. In the

7. See Richard Conklin, "The Vatican Challenges Catholic Academia's Declaration of Independence," *Notre Dame Magazine* (Summer 1986) 43–44.

8. *Origins* 20:9 (June 1990).

spring and fall of 1986, seven of the twelve seminaries of the Episcopal Church passed resolutions warning of the consequences for Church unity of the developing policy toward dissent within the Roman Catholic Church.[9]

In a unanimous statement of May 23, 1986, the faculty of the General Theological Seminary in New York City wrote of its concern:

> The question as we perceive it now is whether or not the Anglican Communion should envision closer ecumenical relations with a church that seems officially determined to suppress public discussion, debate, dialogue, and even disagreement on major theological issues that face the church especially when they are raised by those who teach in its institutions of higher learning and priestly formation . . . the Vatican's treatment of Professor Curran raises a fresh and grave threat for Christian intellectual freedom and ecumenical credibility. . . .[10]

The School of Theology of the University of the South, on September 22, 1986, passed unanimously a "statement of concern" about Episcopal Church relations with the Roman Catholic Church which included the following:

> We affirm that the broader issue of free theological inquiry and its relationship to ecclesiastical authority is an important item that needs to be addressed directly in the course of the continuing Anglican–Roman Catholic dialogue.[11]

On September 23, 1986, the faculty of the Episcopal Divinity School in Cambridge issued a statement that echoed these concerns about academic freedom and their implications for the dialogue:

> We are frankly dismayed at what Father Curran's dismissal from the theological faculty of Catholic University may signal for the future of ecumenical dialogue between Roman and Anglican scholars. We echo the concern of our colleagues at the General Seminary as to whether a credible ecumenical dialogue can survive proscriptions against honest intellectual inquiry in theological scholarship and teaching.[12]

A statement on September 30, 1986, from the faculty of the Virginia Theological Seminary in Alexandria, warns of the impact of these develop-

9. These responses have been surveyed in two articles in the *Journal of Ecumenical Studies* 23:2 (Spring 1986) 354, and 23:4 (Fall 1986) 788.

10. "Open Letter to the Members of ARCIC II," *Journal of Ecumenical Studies* 23:2 (Spring 1986) 354.

11. "Episcopal Seminary Reactions Continue," *Journal of Ecumenical Studies* 23:4 (Fall 1986) 788.

12. *Idem.*

ments on local ecumenical cooperation, if they are "received" and continued:

> This matter is of particular concern to our Faculty, since we are members of the Washington Theological Consortium, along with the Department of Theology at Catholic University. . . . Like our colleagues at General Seminary, we heartily approve of the closer relations and profited greatly from our participation in the Consortium and from the resulting covenant relation with the Dominican House of Studies. We are deeply disturbed, however, by the possible effect of the action of the Vatican on such cooperative academic ventures in the future.[13]

A similar statement on October 17, 1986, from the Episcopal Seminary of the Southwest in Austin, looked with caution and concern to the future:

> It is to be noted that this action follows on the ARCIC *Final Report* where substantial agreement in a number of doctrinal areas was achieved. Differences on matters of authority—its nature, exercise and implications—in the Church were recognized. . . . These questions have yet to be discussed in the conversations between Anglicans and Roman Catholics. The answers to these questions and related issues have an inescapable bearing on the future of ecumenical relations between our two Churches.[14]

Perhaps the longest and most thoughtful warning of the consequences of the Roman direction, if it continued to be "received," came from the Church Divinity School of the Pacific, at the very end of 1986:

> A unity by fiat will not convince; a clarity by coercion will not hide the unfinished debate. Official Catholic moral teaching may thus lose standing in the private deliberations of conscience, and will surely lose stature in the Christian academic community. We value our shared tradition too much not to decry such consequences . . . we count on your Commission to do all it can to restore a positive context to our common discussions on these and other important issues.[15]

The last of these statements came in 1987 from the faculty of Nashotah House in Wisconsin. It said in part:

> The line of thinking from Rome on theological dissent undermines seriously the work of ARCIC on Authority and Ministry in the Church. . . . We would therefore find it difficult to imagine how we might accept the universal jurisdiction over other bishops, claimed

13. *Ibid.*, 789.
14. *Idem.*
15. *Ibid.*, 790–791.

for the Bishop of Rome, as it has been exercised in cases of dissent, and as it might be exercised in other cases. We urge ARCIC and ARC to discuss these matters openly and honestly, for we believe them to be most serious and fundamental barriers to our hope for unity with the Roman Catholic Church.[16]

Conclusion

It is clear, then, that the line of thinking on dissent now developing within the Roman Catholic Church has not been received by Episcopalians and that the Vatican's moves in these areas over the last decade have generated great concern among leaders within the Episcopal community. The issue of dissent might appear to be a purely internal matter for the Roman Catholic Church. However, in Curran's case, the offending views are fairly moderate expressions of opinions stated much more strongly by most Episcopalians. For example, when Curran accepts the legitimacy of contraception, he uses language that most Episcopalians would consider mild. By repudiating him on that point, the Vatican emphasizes its disagreement with most Episcopalians. Similarly, when it rejects Hans Küng's understanding of the relationship between infallible teaching and more flexible expressions of Church doctrine, the Vatican repudiates Küng at a point where his understanding is conservative by Anglican standards. The result is to deepen the disagreements between Rome and Anglicans on the teaching role and authority of the church. This, as all the Episcopal seminary statements have pointed out, seems to be reversing a post-Vatican II trend toward mutual understanding of perennially divisive issues of ecclesiology. These are matters of deep concern: for the new line on dissent within the Roman Catholic Church and the refusal of the Episcopal Church to "receive" this development is leading to a crisis of confidence in the method and purpose of the ecumenical enterprise.

16. "A Statement from the Dean and Faculty of Nashotah House Concerning Recent Actions in the Roman Catholic Church," February 1987.

PRIESTHOOD
AND
COMMUNITY

11

Priests

Transitions and Traditions

ARCIC I revolutionized relations between Roman Catholics and Anglicans because it revealed substantial agreement on critical areas of Eucharistic doctrine and the understanding of ordained ministry. Both churches are faithful to the threefold structure of bishop, priest, and deacon. Both affirm the doctrine of apostolic succession. ARCIC I reported that agreement had been reached on

> the essentials of Eucharistic faith with regard to the sacramental presence of Christ and the sacrificial dimension of the Eucharist, and on the nature and purpose of priesthood, ordination and apostolic succession.[1]

It was ARCIC I's substantial agreement on Eucharistic doctrine which really set the stage for agreement on ordained ministry. The commission deliberately focused on the doctrines of Eucharistic sacrifice and the real presence—both historically areas of controversy. The participants agreed on the absolute sufficiency, once-for-all character and uniqueness of Christ's sacrifice upon the cross. Christ's atoning work is made present and effective in the life of the contemporary church through the celebration of the Eucharist.

The key term here is *anamnesis* or memorial. According to 1 Corinthians 11:24-25 and Luke 22:19, Jesus' words were: "Do this as a memorial (*anamnesin*) of me." *Anamnesis* is a more far-reaching concept than is implied by its English translation, "memorial." *Anamnesis* refers to the making present of a past event. Thus when the Israelites celebrated Passover at the time of Christ, they experienced themselves as somehow present at the original exodus event. In the same way, Christ's atoning death upon the cross is made really present for us in the Eucharist.

---

1. *The Final Report*, 44.

Both churches perceive the action of the president at the Eucharist, reciting the words of Christ at the Last Supper, and distributing the holy gifts of bread and wine, as standing in sacramental relation to what Christ himself did in offering his life as a sacrifice for the whole world. For both churches, the Eucharist is the central action by which we recall Christ's self-offering.

On September 13, 1896, *Apostolicae Curae,* a papal letter, had condemned Anglican Orders as "absolutely null and utterly void," due in part to a perceived deficiency in Anglicanism's doctrine of Eucharistic sacrifice. At Vatican Council II (1962–65), however, several of the council fathers called for a reexamination of that judgment. In 1978 the Vatican archives were opened through the year 1903, and revealed that four of the eight members of the "Apostolic Commission" that investigated Anglican orders prior to the publication of *Apostolicae Curae* had advised the pope in favor of recognizing Anglican orders. ARCIC I's substantial agreement on Eucharistic theology, including "the sacrificial dimension of the Eucharist," now placed the issue of Anglican priesthood in a new light, opening the way for joint discussion of the ordained ministry.[2]

For both churches, the call to ordained ministry derives from God but is recognized by the church. It is the *koinonia* or community which discerns the appropriateness of the perceived call. Thus ordination is not a personal right but an act of commissioning by the church.

Episcopalians and Roman Catholics agree on the structure of the ordained ministry. Oversight of the community—*episcopé*—is entrusted to the local bishop. It is the bishop's task to lead the Church in being faithful to the apostolic faith, in living out that faith in the life of the contemporary church, and in transmitting that faith to the church of the future. The bishop, as chief pastor of the diocese, together with representative clergy, sets aside presbyters—or priests—for the ongoing ministry of local congregations. The presbyters share in the bishop's oversight of the church and celebrate the ministry of word and sacraments. In the bishop's absence a presbyter presides at the Eucharist and pronounces absolution. Deacons, who traditionally report to the bishop, assist both bishops and presbyters in their ministries of word, sacraments, and oversight. Deacons are particularly charged with ministry in and to the world at large.

The measure of theological agreement on Eucharistic doctrine and ordained ministry is extremely encouraging. It has helped deepen the sense of community between our two churches to such an extent that we are

---

2. *Origins* 20:9 (1990) 136; see George H. Tavard, *A Review of Anglican Orders: The Problem and the Solutions* (Collegeville: The Liturgical Press, 1990); also R. William Franklin and George H. Tavard, "Commentary on ARC/USA Statement on Anglican Orders," *Journal of Ecumenical Studies* 27:2 (190) 261–287.

increasingly able to reexamine our continuing difficulties. Some of these are raised in this chapter.

Considerable anxiety has arisen from the Episcopal Church's decision to ordain women as priests and bishops. This is contrary to the stated belief and practice of the Roman Catholic Church, yet there has been strong support for such a move among some Roman Catholics in the United States. On the other hand, a relatively small but undeniably faithful number of Episcopalians questions the theological appropriateness of ordaining women as priest and bishop.

Episcopalians have been disturbed by what is termed the "Pastoral Provision." This has permitted Episcopal priests, after thorough examination, to be ordained as Roman Catholic priests. Sometimes married clergy who bring their congregations with them continue as the priests in the parishes they had served as Episcopalians, using a modified form of the Book of Common Prayer. This measure has troubled some married former Roman Catholic priests who wish that similar provision could be made for them. It also raises questions in the minds of faithful celibate priests who would choose to marry were canon law changed on this point.

On the other hand, many former Roman Catholic priests have been accepted into the Episcopal Church. A desire to marry appears often to have been a major reason for their transfer. Some Roman Catholics have questioned the ease with which many such transfers apparently occur, and we should note that their concern has sometimes been paralleled by Episcopalians, who have asked whether such transfers truly represent a conversion to the faith and practice of Anglicanism.

This section addresses matters which are on the cutting edge of debate both between and within our churches. Our *koinonia* makes possible honest criticism and diligent questioning. It is in this spirit that we address our topic of ordained ministry and community.

12

Ordination of Women

Reception

In 1944 Florence Tim Oi Li became the first woman ordained to the Anglican priesthood. The Right Reverend R. O. Hall, bishop of Hong Kong, ordained her, having first received permission from the local synod. The exceptional pastoral circumstances caused by World War II were the reason for this break with tradition. The archbishops of Canterbury and York repudiated her ordination, and Florence Tim Oi Li voluntarily ceased to exercise her orders.

The next women priests ordained in the Anglican Communion were also from Hong Kong. The ordinations of the Reverend Jane Hwang and the Reverend Joyce Bennett took place in 1971. Although their ordinations led to criticism from various areas of the Anglican communion, their validity has never been officially challenged.

Extraordinary pastoral circumstances led to the ordination of the first woman priest in Hong Kong. By contrast the ordination of women to the priesthood of the Episcopal Church in the United States was the culmination of a broadly based movement seeking a representative role for women in the Church.[1] As late as the 1960s, men and women were effectively segregated in their roles in the church. In almost half the dioceses, only men could serve on vestry or as deputies to diocesan convention. (The vestry, of which the rector is a member, is the governing body in each local congregation; diocesan convention is the decision making body of the diocese.) Only men could serve on General Convention—the national church's triennial decision-making body. Women invariably had to ex-

---

1. The following texts were of particular help in preparing this discussion: Mary S. Donovan, *Women Priests in the Episcopal Church* (Cincinnati: Forward Movement Press, 1988) 3–28; David E. Sumner, *The Episcopal Church's History 1945–85* (Wilton, Conn.: Morehouse-Barlow, 1987) 7–30; John Booty, *The Episcopal Church in Crisis* (Cambridge, Mass.: Cowley Publications, 1988) 65–72; and Sara Maitland, *A Map of the New Country: Women and Christianity* (London: Routlege & Kegan Paul, 1983).

press their call within the church through traditional "female" roles within such groups as the Episcopal Church Women and the Altar Guild.

In the General Conventions of 1970 and 1973, motions to enable women to be ordained as priest were narrowly defeated. At that point opinion was divided on how next to proceed. A group declared that "the democratic process, the political dynamics, and the legal guidelines" were "out of step with the divine imperative which says, now is the time."[2]

On July 29, 1974, eleven women deacons were ordained to the priesthood of the Episcopal Church in Philadelphia. In a joint statement they answered critics who saw women's ordination as nothing more than an aspect of the women's liberation movement. The women ordained in Philadelphia sought to "reaffirm and recover the universality of Christ's ministry as symbolized in that order [priesthood]."[3] Their action stemmed from their sacramental theology.

Four more women were ordained priest in Washington, D.C., on September 7, 1975. The 1976 General Convention decided that women could be ordained to the priesthood and episcopate. This ruling, which took effect on January 1, 1977, was a major step in the Episcopal Church's reception of the doctrine that women and men should share equally in all facets of the ordained ministry.

The reception of doctrine is more than the official actions of church assemblies or the church leadership. It goes beyond the pronouncements of theologians. Doctrine has to become part of the church's ongoing life. The faithful have to receive it. The Episcopal Church found that it was one thing to ordain women to the priesthood and another for parishes to invite women into the fullness of parish ministry.

By June 1987, 69 percent of all clergymen and 56 percent of all clergywomen of the Episcopal Church were registered with the Church Deployment Office. Of those men and women ordained after January 1, 1977, 46 percent of the men and only 19 percent of the women served as rectors or vicars of parishes. The position was reversed for assistants or associates in parishes: women numbered 46 percent and men 36 percent. Only as chaplains was there a higher percentage of women than men: women numbering 9 percent and men 4 percent.[4] By 1987 women made up 39 percent of the students in the Episcopal seminaries studying for the mas-

2. Paul Washington, "Address to the Congregation," Episcopal Church of the Advocate, Philadelphia, July 24, 1974 (cited in Donovan, 7). Paul Washington would later preach at Barbara Harris' consecration as bishop.

3. Donovan, 8, citing "An Open Letter," July 20, 1974, signed by the eleven women ordained priest.

4. Donovan, 22–23, presents these figures from two computer searches made by the Church Deployment Office, June 15, 1987.

ter of divinity degree, the normal academic requirement for ordination in the Episcopal Church.[5] This trend suggests that bishops and their diocesan commissions on ministry—the body which screens ordination candidates for the diocesan bishop—have increasingly accepted females as suitable candidates for the church's ordained ministry.

Participation of Women

In 1987 the Committee for the Full Participation of Women in the [Episcopal] Church published an action research study entitled *Reaching for Wholeness: The Participation of Women in the Episcopal Church.* It was prepared for distribution at the 1988 General Convention. It notes that "of the approximately 825 women who were priests at the end of 1987, 200 (24 percent) were in charge of congregations: 41 percent of those were vicars and 59 percent were rectors."[6]

If we add figures for 1988, published by the Episcopal Church's Office for Women in Mission and Ministry,[7] we find a steady increase in women holding positions as rectors, vicars, associates, and assistants. Between 1982 and 1988 the number of women rectors rose from 24 to 127, the number of women vicars rose from 34 to 93, and the numbers of women serving as associates or assistants rose from 220 to 647. At that time one woman, Geralyn Wolf, served as a cathedral dean, and 35 ordained women served on cathedral staffs.

The following table indicates a steady increase in ordained women in all these areas. (Unfortunately numbers are not available for 1986):

	1982	1983	1984	1985	1987	1988
Rectors	24	34	47	70	117	127
Vicars	34	44	60	66	83	93
Assoc/ Assistants	222	226	363	434	533	647

From 1982 to 1988 female associates and assistants increased by just over 2.9 times and vicars by just over 2.7 times. Rectorships held by women increased at nearly twice these rates, almost 5.3 times. More recent, but less detailed figures were distributed at the July 1991 General Convention

5. Donovan, 9.

6. *Reaching,* 54.

7. Ann Smith and the Office of Women in Mission and Ministry provide the most up-to-date data on the ordination of women in the Episcopal Church. The most recent statistics on the ordination of women in the Anglican communion were released on March 25, 1992. At that point there were two women consecrated to the episcopate, 1,342 women ordained to the priesthood, 1,942 women ordained to the diaconate.

of the Episcopal Church. These recorded that over 300 women were in charge of congregations as rectors, vicars, priests-in-charge, interim priests, or as co-pastors. About 650 women deacons and priests serve as assistant or associate priests. In all, between 12 and 13 percent of the Episcopal Church's 15,000 clergy are women.

Reception Within the Episcopal Church

The steady increase in women rectors between 1982 and 1988 suggests that the Episcopal Church has begun the process of receiving women's ordination as a sacramental practice in accord with its own life. Yet the low percentage (10 percent) of ordained women in the Episcopal Church suggests the provisional character of this reception.

It is sometimes claimed that the ordination of women has led to a drop in membership in the Episcopal Church—a sign that the practice is not being accepted. The Office of Women in Mission and Ministry refutes this assertion in an undated fact sheet entitled *Ordination of Women*, which deals with figures up to May 11, 1988.

During the first decade of ordaining women, attendance at Episcopal churches increased about 28 percent. In 1974 the average attendance at four key services was 884,358. In 1985 it was 1,136,131. (These figures are culled from reports to the National Church which request figures for four key services each year.) In addition, there was a paralleled increase in pledged income during that period. This adds support to the conclusion that the Episcopal Church is receiving the ordination of women—however provisionally—into its life.

According to Bishop Donald Parsons, the number of those communicants who have left the Episcopal Church "has not been overwhelming" but "those departing were dedicated and active communicants."[8] Of these, some have left for other traditions. Some laity and clergy have become a part of breakaway Anglican churches. A number have remained within the Episcopal Church while affiliating with a voluntary association of dioceses and areas termed the Episcopal Synod of America. (According to its constitution, the Episcopal Synod of America is committed to upholding evangelical faith and catholic order within Anglicanism. The Synod, which was founded at Fort Worth, Texas, June 3, 1989, opposes the ordination of women as priests and bishops.)

By the time of the 1994 General Convention of the Episcopal Church, all but a handful of the dioceses of the Episcopal Church were ordaining women to the priesthood. A resolution concerning the ordination of women was passed in both the House of Bishops and the House of Depu-

8. For Bishop Parsons' comments, see Donovan, 174–175.

ties. This resolution reaffirmed Canon, Title III.8.i, "guaranteeing both men and women access to the ordination process in this Church." It recognized that "women are not ordained to the priesthood in all dioceses at this time," and that "those who support and those who oppose the ordination of women each hold a recognized theological opinion in this Church." The key instruction of the resolution, however, was as follows: "The Presiding Bishop and the President of the House of Deputies, in consultation with two bishops, whom they shall designate, from the dioceses where such ordinations do not occur, appoint a committee to promote dialogue and understanding and to discuss how the canon can be implemented in every diocese of this Church."

In an earlier draft of this resolution the word "addressed" was used rather than "implemented." The final choice of the stronger term, "implemented," and the adoption of "implemented" by both houses, indicates that the Episcopal Church is continuing to receive the ordination of women as an authentic expression of its doctrine and ministry.

The First Female Seminary Dean

On July 1, 1994, a little more than two months before the 1994 General Convention met, the Reverend Martha J. Horne became the first woman to head a seminary of the Episcopal Church. Her election as dean and president of the Virginia Theological Seminary was announced on May 18, 1994, after a search committee had considered some sixty names from five Anglican provinces. Virginia Seminary, of which Martha Horne is an alumna, is currently the largest seminary in the Episcopal Church and the second oldest. The Very Reverend Martha Horne's election to this crucial office in the training of candidates for ordained ministry indicates the continuing reception of the ministry of women clergy throughout the Episcopal Church's structure.

Women Bishops

As women priests became a visible presence in the Episcopal Church, churchgoers increasingly asked when we would see the first woman bishop. In September 1985, the House of Bishops of the Episcopal Church passed a resolution expressing its intention not to withhold consent to the election of a bishop on the grounds of gender. The Episcopal Church also sought the advice of the Anglican episcopate at large by placing the question before a meeting of the primates of the communion when they met in March 1986, in Toronto. The primates meeting approached this as a matter of consultation in order that the Episcopal Church's decision should be as fully informed as possible. In no sense was the matter interpreted as a request from the Episcopal Church to go ahead.

A report on *Women and the Episcopate* was prepared for the 1988 Lambeth Conference. This report stressed the need for provinces to listen to each other and understand what was being said by those who held different views. The report said this about the process of reception, were a province to ordain a woman as bishop:

> The development should be offered to the Anglican Communion in an open process of reception.
>
> The development could not be expressed as the mind of the Church until it were accepted by the whole Communion. Even then there would necessarily be a tentativeness about it until it were accepted by the universal church.
>
> Consideration of the ordination of women to the presbyterate and episcopate within the Communion would need to continue with Provinces listening to one another's thoughts and experiences, aiding one another in theological reflection and exercising mutual sensitivity and care.
>
> Debate in the wider fellowship of the Churches ought to be encouraged, particularly within existing bilateral and multi-lateral dialogues.[9]

The Lambeth 1988 document *Dogmatic and Pastoral Concerns* commented that no province which ordains women has seen this to be a complete breach with the past. It is neither intended nor seen as a repudiation of Scripture or sacramental order. The arguments for women's ordination have been recognizably Christian and recognizably Anglican. Importantly, "At the level of its official voice, Anglicanism as such does not hold this development to be so damaging to the common discipline of Scripture and sacraments that it cannot be lived with."[10]

Barbara Harris' election on September 24, 1988, as suffragan bishop of Massachusetts was a highly significant sign of increasing acceptance of women's ordination within the Episcopal Church. Election to the episcopate in the Episcopal Church is a long and thorough process. Usually a search committee ascertains the needs of the diocese and shifts through a large list of nominees. Eventually this committee presents its final list of nominees to the diocesan convention. Invariably other names can either be nominated by a specified process prior to the election or be received from the floor. Once the election has taken place in the local diocese, it has to be confirmed by a majority vote in favor by the standing committees and bishops with jurisdiction throughout the Episcopal Church. Thus

9. The Lambeth Conference 1988, *The Truth Shall Make You Free* (London: Church House, 1988) 115–116.

10. *Ibid.*, 116.

all orders of the church, ordained and lay, are involved in the process. This is the first step in receiving the ministry of the bishop-elect.

Bishop Harris was duly elected by this inclusive process. The election itself took over eight ballots. Harris came second on the first ballot, but on the eighth ballot she was duly elected by a majority of both clergy and lay votes.

The consent process was sometimes controversial, but on January 3, 1989, Barbara Harris received the majority of consents needed from the House of Bishops. She was consecrated on February 11, 1989, with the Reverend Florence Tim Oi Li, then in her eighties, among those present. The strength of support for Barbara Harris' election was apparent when 55 bishops stretched their hands over Barbara Harris at her consecration as the the first women and 834th bishop of the Episcopal Church in the United States. Since then she has maintained a busy calendar of official acts, including participation in the consecration of other bishops. This confirms that her ministry is being received within the Episcopal Church.

Any attempt to gage the Episcopal Church's reception of the ordination of women to the priesthood and episcopate should be set in the larger context of the Anglican communion. Lambeth's 1988 report on *Dogmatic and Pastoral Concerns* warned that reception is not just about "response and affirmation in word but entails embodying what is affirmed in the life of the community." It notes that reception "is a gradual and dynamic process."[11] Reception takes time, and there is an inevitable "provisionality" about decisions taken by synods and councils of the Church. Reception is clearly by the whole People of God in that decisions which have been accepted and acted upon by provincial synods and endorsed by a majority of bishops at Lambeth can still be modified or reversed. As such the Episcopal Church is still living in a provisional situation with regard to the acceptance of women as priests and bishops, but a provisional situation in which such ordinations are becoming increasingly accepted by the church at large. While we cannot yet claim that the Episcopal Church has received the ordination of women as priest and bishop, it is clear that the Church's movement is more toward reception than non-reception.

The 1988 Lambeth Conference of Bishops passed a resolution asking the archbishop of Canterbury to appoint a commission to examine relationships between the various provinces of the Anglican communion, particularly in light of the ordination of women to the episcopate. The Most Reverend Robert Eames, primate of all Ireland and metropolitan, chaired this commission which produced its *Report of the Archbishop of Canterbury's Commission on Communion and Women in the Episcopate.* The commission received as its mandate "to discover how Anglicans can live

11. *Ibid.,* 117.

in the highest possible degree of communion with differences of principle and practice on the ordination of women to the episcopate.''[12]

A key concept in this report is "provisionality." Reception of necessity is an open process. The Anglican Communion, under the guidance of the Holy Spirit, is engaged either in receiving or not receiving the ministry of women as priests and bishops. The Eames Report suggests that Anglicans recognize that an unhappy consequence of Christianity's current division is that there is no church whose ordained ministry is not in some way questioned by another. At this time, Anglicans who are troubled by the decision to ordain women as priests and bishops are exhorted to live sacrificially with this provisional situation "until this development is more fully received within the Anglican Communion and the universal Church."[13] Thus dissent is permissible, but it is to be a limited dissent:

> Dissenting priests and congregations must, for their part, not go so far as to refuse canonical recognition to their diocesan bishop or to say that they are not in communion with their ordinary. This would mean that their positions would have to fall short of maintaining that the Church could never admit women to the priesthood or episcopate.[14]

The Eames Report is concerned to maintain the unity of the church. It cites approvingly the position of St. Cyprian:

> . . . in the event of disagreement no compulsion should be brought to bear upon the dissident bishop or bishops. The Church, while still preserving unity, will be obliged to live for a time with the fact of disagreement (Letter 55).[15]

Implications of the Gospel, a joint report of the Lutheran-Episcopalian dialogue in the United States, indicated the extent to which Episcopalians are receiving the ordination of women as priests and bishops as a practice consistent with the life of their church. Presidency at the Eucharist, the report claims, is not about gender. The New Testament neither identifies the function of the twelve apostles as presiding at the Eucharist nor identifies maleness as a quality which is necessary for those who preside at the Eucharist.[16]

---

12. *Report of the Archbishop of Canterbury's Commission on Communion and Women in the Episcopate 1989,* by Robert Eames, Chairman (London: Church House, 1989) 7.

13. *Ibid.,* 13.

14. *Ibid.,* 20.

15. *Ibid.,* 23.

16. William A. Norgren and William G. Rusch, eds., *Implications of the Gospel,* Lutheran–Episcopal Dialogue, Series III Minneapolis (Augsburg and Cincinnati: Forward Movement Publications, 1988) cited by Eames Report, 30.

Soon the Church in New Zealand joined the Episcopal Church in selecting a woman bishop. Just over a year after Barbara Harris became the first woman bishop in the Anglican communion, the Church in New Zealand elected the Reverend Penelope Jamieson as Anglicanism's first woman diocesan bishop. Dr. Jamieson was consecrated and installed as the seventh bishop of Dunedin on June 29, 1990.

There are dissimilarities between Harris and Jamieson. Harris is black and thus also represents an ethnic minority in the United States. Jamieson is white and was born in England. Questions were raised about Harris' lack of a theological degree; Jamieson has a B.D. and a Ph.D. Harris was elected a suffragan, and Jamieson a diocesan bishop. Their very dissimilarities confirm a growing movement in the Episcopal Church to accept women as bishops as well as priests in different churches within the Anglican Communion. This conclusion is supported by the subsequent election of three further female bishops: Jane Holmes Dixon as suffragan bishop of Washington; Mary Adelia McLeod as diocesan bishop of Vermont; and Virginia Matthews as suffragan bishop of Toronto.

Jane Holmes Dixon was elected bishop suffragan of Washington on May 30, 1992. Jane Dixon received her seminary degree in 1981 and held two appointments as an associate, one in the diocese of Virginia and one in the diocese of Washington before becoming rector of St. Philip's Church, Laurel, Maryland, in 1986. At the time of her election, Jane Dixon was president of the Standing Committee of the diocese of Washington.

Jane Dixon was elected from among a list of seven nominees. She received the highest number of votes cast in every ballot in both the house of clergy and the house of laity. Despite the number of nominees, it took only three ballots for her election. Since Jane Dixon had served her ordained ministry first in the neighboring diocese of Virginia, and then in the Washington diocese, and had been a prominent lay person in the diocese of Washington prior to that, her election is most naturally interpreted as a clear endorsement of her call to the episcopate by the people of the Episcopal diocese of Washington. The election of Jane Dixon is a further step in the Episcopal Church's reception of women as priest and bishop.

On June 5, 1993, the Reverend Mary Adelia McLeod, who received her seminary degree in 1980, was elected diocesan bishop of Vermont on the third ballot. Her consecration took place on November 1, 1993, and is especially significant as the first election of a female as a diocesan bishop in the Episcopal Church. By the end of the year, with the election of Virginia Matthews, the Anglican Church of Canada became the third Anglican province to elect a female as bishop. The elections of Dixon, McLeod, and Matthews are further indications of the growing reception of women as priest and bishop in the Episcopal Church and within the provinces of the Anglican Communion.

Roman Catholic Non-Reception

While the Episcopal Church appears, however slowly, to be receiving the doctrine that women share in the fullness of the priesthood and episcopate, the Roman Catholic Church has repudiated what it considers a major breach of tradition.

On July 9, 1975, Donald Coggan, then archbishop of Canterbury, wrote to Pope Paul VI about "the slow but steady growth of a consensus of opinion within the Anglican Communion that there are no fundamental objections in principle to the ordination of women to the priesthood."[17] The pope, in a letter dated November 30, 1975, reiterated the Roman Catholic Church's conviction that "it is not admissible to ordain women to the priesthood for very fundamental reasons."[18] Scripture records that Jesus chose only men as his apostles. This has been the constant practice of the Church in imitation of Christ, and there is the Roman Catholic Church's "living teaching authority which has consistently held that the exclusion of women from the priesthood is in accordance with God's plan for his church."[19]

At the close of the Lambeth Conference 1988, Archbishop Runcie and Pope John Paul II exchanged correspondence.[20] The archbishop recorded the conference's very positive response to ARCIC I, but concentrated upon the question of women's ordination. He advised that, despite some division over the issue, some Anglican provinces might soon ordain women to the episcopate. The conference had resolved to respect such a decision, together with the pain of some impaired communion, rather than risk schism.

Pope John Paul II's response made plain his objections. The 1988 Lambeth Conference's position on women's ordination had added a new complexity to Anglican–Roman Catholic relations. ARCIC II had been charged with studying "all that hinders the mutual recognition of the ministries of our Communions." Now, the pope wrote:

> The ordination of women to the priesthood in some provinces of the Anglican Communion, together with the recognition of the right of individual provinces to proceed with the ordination of women to the episcopacy, appears to preempt this study and effectively block the path to the mutual recognition of ministries.

17. See Joseph W. Witmer and J. Robert Wright, eds., *Called to Full Unity, Documents on Anglican–Roman Catholic Relations 1966–1983* (Washington: Office of Publishing and Promotion Services, United States Catholic Conference, 1986) 132.

18. *Ibid.,* 133.

19. *Idem.*

20. Eames Report, 34–39.

> The Catholic Church . . . is firmly opposed to this development, viewing it as a break with Tradition of a kind we have no competence to authorize.[21]

The pope's comments indicate that the Roman Catholic Church stands by its belief that women cannot be ordained to the priesthood—or episcopate—of the Catholic Church. Thus this becomes a clear case of the Roman Catholic Church's non-reception of a doctrine and practice which is becoming increasingly accepted within Anglicanism.

Where does the issue go from here? There is a clear need to discuss our particular understandings of tradition. We need to ask specifically whether tradition presents incontrovertible evidence on whether women can be bishops and priests. ARCIC II is continuing its dialogue. In their episcopal elections at least some dioceses of the Episcopal Church are continuing to consider women candidates, some of whom have made the final list of candidates.

Reception Within the Anglican Communion

The Church of England, which other communions and churches so often look to first in considering Anglicanism has now voted officially on November 11, 1992 to proceed to the ordination of women as priests. In 1990 England had eight hundred women deacons, and when these women are ordained as priests there will be no shortage of candidates. 1990 also saw a report titled *Episcopal Ministry* commissioned by the archbishops of Canterbury and York. The report reveals division among its members on women's ordination, yet it affirms the members' determination "to maintain the highest degree of communion in spite of differences of opinion and also practice."[22] Above all, *Episcopal Ministry* is encouraged by the proper role of leadership which the episcopate of the Anglican communion has taken in trying to work through this issue without resorting either to quick solutions or to schism.

Reception of women as bishops and priests in the Episcopal Church is a practice which has become increasingly accepted into the life of the Episcopal Church. Has the ordination of women as bishops and priests been received by the church as a measure of its life? Certainly not in the four dioceses where the bishop does not ordain women to these orders. Throughout the Anglican communion the issue still excites considerable and often heated debate. It is difficult, therefore, to claim that the church has yet received the ordination of women as priests and bishops as a meas-

21. *Ibid.,* 37–38.

22. *Episcopal Ministry,* The Report of the Archbishops' Group on the Episcopate 1990 (London: Church House Publishing, 1990) 260.

ure of its own life, but we can legitimately claim that the Episcopal Church is moving in the direction of receiving women's ordination as a legitimate ecclesiological development consistent with tradition.

Conclusion

Our study indicates a slow but steady movement in the Episcopal Church toward receiving women as priests and bishops. Pope John Paul II's letter of December 8, 1988, to Archbishop Runcie stated the Roman Catholic Church's opposition to this development, viewing it as a break with tradition. Therefore the official positions of the Episcopal Church and the Roman Catholic Church differ on whether women can legitimately be ordained as priests and bishops. Neither church is currently receiving the other's position as its own.

13

Ordination of Women

Non-Reception

Koinonia, the church as communion, the church as a communion of communions, is a unifying principle of ARCIC I and II.[1] A severe test of this unifying concept, both within and between the Anglican and Roman Catholic Churches, is the admission or prohibition of women to the ministerial priesthood and to the episcopacy. Decisions on women as priests and bishops place in sharpest focus the two concepts of this study, communion and reception.

The Anglican communion holds within its communion both churches which admit women to priesthood and episcopacy and churches which do not. Anglican churches, both those which prescribe and those which prohibit the ordination of women, strive to retain communion with members who have not received the official position of their churches. The tension between those who favor and those who disapprove of the ordination of women is also felt within the Roman Catholic Church. From the ecumenical perspective of the two churches, there is the challenge to continue to move toward fuller communion with each other when they hold opposing positions on this question.

We have defined reception as that process in which, under the guidance of the Holy Spirit, Anglicans and Roman Catholics at every level of church life discern elements of praxis, spirituality, doctrine, and discipline in one another's churches—in whole or in part—as authentic expressions of the Gospel and of the apostolic faith. Reception and non-reception at every level of church life—of statements, strategies, correspondence, organizations, publications, and actions, both official and non-official—contribute to the story of the ordination and prohibition of women to the priestly ministry. Though the stories differ, both the Anglican and Roman Catholic communions have had to discern as authen-

---

1. See *The Final Report,* "Introduction," n. 5–8, and ARCIC II's report, "Church as Communion," *Catholic International* 2:7 (April 1–14, 1991) 2.

tic expressions of Gospel and apostolic faith elements of praxis, spirituality, doctrine, and discipline as they have approved or prohibited the ordination of women.

The Challenge

In the 1970s the Episcopal Church ordained women to the priesthood and the Roman Catholic Church made an official pronouncement prohibiting ordination of women to the priestly ministry. These actions moved both churches into ever deepening and widening considerations of basic Christian teaching on the ordained priesthood, priesthood of the baptized, Eucharist, baptism, sacrament, symbol, church, tradition, Christology, Christian anthropology, and images of God.[2] For our purpose we limit our considerations to a brief examination of the nature and subject of the presbyterate.

Both communions agree that a permanent character is received at ordination and that this makes priesthood more than a function. That one remains a deacon, priest, or bishop even if one does not perform diaconal, priestly, or episcopal services is the teaching of each church.[3] There are, nevertheless, questions concerning each communion's understanding of the term *in persona Christi*,[4] which specifically relate to the focus of our study, the subject of ordination. The official decision of the Episcopal Church to admit women to priesthood and episcopacy indicates that this branch of the Anglican communion considers that women as well as men can receive the priestly character at ordination. Thus a female priest, in the same manner as a male priest, signifies one dimension of Christ in the Eucharist.[5] The current Roman Catholic understanding of Christian anthropology seems to imply that women, unlike men, are in their very nature unable to receive at ordination the priestly character which would enable them to signify Christ in the Eucharist. Roman Catholic law (canon 1024) also states that the subject of a valid ordination must be male.

After this brief contextualization we examine the reception rather than the content of the Roman Catholic statement[6] on the ordination of women.

2. See the Guide to Further Reading in this volume for treatment of these topics in relation to ordination of women.

3. See *The Final Report,* "Ministry and Ordination," n. 15.

4. See *The Ordination of Women to the Priesthood. A Second Report by the House of Bishops of the General Synod the Church of England* (London: General Synod of the Church of England Church House) 29–30, n. 58–60.

5. *Ibid.,* 34–35, n. 65, n. 66.

6. Congregation for the Doctrine of the Faith, *Declaration on the Question of the Admission of Women to the Ministerial Priesthood, with Commentary* (Washington: United States Catholic Conference, 1977).

We then consider the reception of the prohibition of the ordination of women found in three drafts of a pastoral letter on women by the bishops of the United States.

The Declaration

On October 15, 1976, the Congregation for the Doctrine of the Faith promulgated *A Declaration on the Question of the Admission of Women to the Ministerial Priesthood,* signed by the prefect of the congregation, Franjo Cardinal Seper, and the secretary, Fr. Jerome Hamer, O.P. The accompanying *Commentary* is not signed.

The *Declaration* states clearly that "the Sacred Congregation for the Doctrine of the Faith judges it necessary to recall that the Church, in fidelity to the example of the Lord, does not consider herself authorized to admit women to priestly ministry."[7] The primary reason given for the prohibition is tradition. "The Catholic Church has never felt that priestly or episcopal ordination can be validly conferred on women."[8] The authority of Scripture is also cited, with some reservations. The scriptural "facts do not make the matter immediately obvious . . . but . . . we have here a number of convergent indications that . . . Jesus did not entrust the apostolic charge to women."[9]

After recalling the norm that priestly ordination is conferred only on men, the *Declaration* reflects on the sacramental nature of Christian priesthood. The *Declaration* indicates that the priest is a sign, a sign that must be perceptible when Christ's role in the Eucharist is to be expressed sacramentally. It states that the "natural resemblance" between Christ and his minister would not exist if the role of Christ were not taken by a man, for Christ himself was and remains a man.[10]

The *Declaration* also states that "the Church, through the voice of her Magisterium . . . decides what can change and what must remain immutable. . . ."[11]

The *Declaration* and to a greater degree the *Commentary* show signs of having been written in response to events in the Church and world. The Latin title of the *Declaration, Inter Insigniores,* is taken from the opening words of the text, "Among the characteristics that mark our present age." This title indicates that the document is a response, or more broadly

7. *Ibid.,* 4.
8. *Ibid.,* 5.
9. *Ibid.,* 7.
10. *Ibid.,* 12.
11. *Ibid.,* 10.

put, a reception or non-reception of the "characteristics of the present day."[12]

Reception and Non-Reception

By locating the reasons for the prohibition of women from ordained ministry in Scripture and tradition, the authors indicate that they have not received some of the historical studies by recent commissions and theologians. Regarding Scripture, the authors of the *Declaration* did not receive the report of the Pontifical Biblical Commission. The commission members agreed unanimously that the New Testament by itself does not seem able to settle in a clear way, and once and for all, whether women can be ordained priests. The members voted twelve to five that scriptural grounds alone are not enough to exclude the possibility of ordaining women.[13] As stated above, the *Declaration* acknowledges that the scriptural position is not immediately obvious. Regarding tradition, some scholars consider the decision not to ordain women a matter of cultural rather than sacred tradition. One author concludes that the church did not confer ordination on women because it absorbed cultural rather than Gospel values.[14] Obviously, this position was not received by the authors of the *Declaration*.

The *Commentary* cites other characteristics of the present age to which the *Declaration* is responding. These include the admission of women to the priesthood in other churches including those that consider that they have preserved the apostolic succession, the correspondence between Pope Paul VI and Archbishop Coggan, the activities of the World Council of Churches, the writings of Catholic scholars, and the Call to Action in Detroit.[15] (The first two have been discussed in the previous chapter.)

Can we discern the *sensus fidelium* regarding the question of the admission of women to the priestly ministry? Have the People of God received this prohibition? The People of God, a concept used by Vatican II to describe the church, includes many overlapping categories of the faithful: lay women and men, theologians, professed religious, priests, deacons, and bishops. We first examine the response to the *Declaration* by the largest group within the Roman Catholic Church, the laity.

12. *Ibid.*, 3.

13. See "Can Women be Priests?" Report from Pontifical Biblical Commission. *Origins* 6:6 (1976) 92–96. See also Carroll Stuelmueller (ed.), *Women and Priesthood,* 235.

14. See George Tavard, *Women in Christianity* (Notre Dame: University of Notre Dame Press, 1973) 227.

15. *Commentary,* 19–21.

Laity. Some surveys indicate that the majority of Roman Catholics in the United States find the ordination of women acceptable[16] but there is also strong opposition to this development by groups such as the Catholic organization, Women for Faith and Families. When we examine actions rather than opinions we find that there is no group which has corporately and publicly left the Roman Catholic Church primarily because it could not accept the prohibition.[17] There have been, however, individual Catholics who have publicly or privately left the church because of the prohibition.[18] Among Catholics who have publicly called their church to open the priesthood to women are the 4,505 persons including laity, religious, priests, and bishops who signed a statement published in the *New York Times,*[19] and such groups as Call to Action and CORPUS.[20] Probably more numerous are those who "receive" the prohibition, that is, make it their own, but either question that it is an authentic expression of the gospel or find the reasons given inadequate.

Theologians. Some theologians responded to the *Declaration* immediately, and many of them found the prohibition, or the reasons for it, less than compelling.[21] Only a few of the publications surveyed for this study defended the prohibition.[22] Apparently few who agree with the prohibition find it necessary to write on the issue. There are also those who find

16. A 1974 poll indicated 29 percent of Catholics favored women priests. A 1985 poll showed 47 percent, and a 1992 Gallup Poll reported that 67 percent favored ordination of women. See Jerry Filteau, "What U.S. Catholics Think," *Catholic News Service* as reported in *The Record* (Louisville: 114, 26 (June 26, 1992) 9.

17. The followers of the late Archbishop Lefebvre accept the prohibition of women priests. Rev. George Stalling's Imani Temple African American Catholic Congregation admits women to priesthood but was formed primarily because of African American concerns.

18. A public personal departure was Mary Daly's symbolic exodus from the Harvard Memorial Chapel in 1971. See Maitland (n. 16) 141.

19. "A Call for Reform in the Catholic Church," *The New York Times,* February 28, 1990, A4.

20. Call to Action, an independent organization of 5,000 laity, religious, and clergy, was formed in 1977 as a Chicago-area response to the United States Bishops' bicentennial "Call to Action" conference in Detroit in 1976. CORPUS (Corps of Reserve Priests for Service) is an association of nearly 11,000 married and celibate priests, laity, and religious sisters and brothers founded in 1974.

21. See faculty of Catholic Theological Union of Chicago: *Women and the Priesthood: Future Directions, A Call to Dialogue* (Collegeville: The Liturgical Press, 1978); Leonard and Arlene Swidler, *Women Priests: A Catholic Commentary on the Vatican Declaration* (New York: Paulist Press, 1977).

22. See Raimondo Spiazzi, et. al., *The Order of Priesthood: Nine Commentaries on the Vatican Decree Inter Insigniores* (Huntington: *Our Sunday Visitor*); David Burell, "The Vatican Declaration: Another View," *America* 136:13 (April 2, 1977) 289.

ordination a questionable goal for women for reasons other than those of the *Declaration*.[23] More recent publications frequently do not focus on the prohibition but place it in the wider context of ministry, women in the church, or feminist spirituality.[24]

Bishops. The *Commentary* states that the document is primarily addressed to bishops, who have the mission of explaining it to their people.[25] Few published texts, however, have been issued by individual bishops. One released on October 7, 1975 (before publication of the *Declaration*) by the secretary of the National Conference of Catholic Bishops discouraged "unreasonable hopes and expectations."[26] Others written after publication uphold the reasons for the prohibition.[27] A few bishops have raised questions and called for more clarity on the church's position.[28] There are no reports of a United States Roman Catholic bishop ordaining a woman. We may conclude that the bishops of the Roman Catholic Church in the United States have received the prohibition on the ordination of women to the priestly ministry.

Drafts of the Bishops' Pastoral on Women[29]

On April 12, 1988, the first draft of a pastoral response by the bishops of the United States to women's concerns was released after extensive hearings. This draft, which frequently quoted the women consulted, was not

23. Anne Kelly and Anne Walsh, "Ordination: A Questionable Goal For Women," *Women and Orders* (New York: Paulist Press, 1974) 67–74.

24. See Anne E. Carr, *Transforming Grace: Christian Tradition and Women's Experience* (San Francisco: Harper & Row, 1988); Carol P. Christ and Judith Plaskow, *Womanspirit Rising* (San Francisco: Harper and Row, 1979) and *Weaving the Vision* (San Francisco: Harper and Row, 1989); Sallie McFague, *Models of God* (Philadelphia: Fortress Press, 1987).

25. *Commentary*, 21.

26. See Joseph Bernardin, "Archbishop Bernardin on Ordination of Women," *N.C. Documentation* (10-3-75).

27. Spiazzi (n. 22) 111–125. Also, Daniel Pilarczyk, "Ordination of Women," *Twelve Tough Issues* (St. Anthony Messenger Press, 1988) 61–66.

28. Jerry Filteau, *Catholic News Service* as reported in "U.S. Bishops Decide to Continue Controversial Women's Pastoral," *The Record* (Louisville: 114, 26 [June 26, 1992] 1, 9).

29. United States Catholic Conference, "Partners in the Mystery of Redemption, A Pastoral Response to Women's Concerns for Church and Society," first draft, *Origins* 17:45 (1988) 759–788; "One in Christ Jesus: A Pastoral Response to the Concerns of Women for Church and Society," second draft, *Origins* 19:44 (1990) 718–740; Proposed Pastoral Response to the Concerns of Women for Church and Society: "Called to be One in Christ Jesus," third draft, *Origins* 21:46 (1992) 762–776.

received by the bishops. After major revisions a second draft, released on April 3, 1990, was not received. A third draft of April 1992, was debated by the bishops in June 1992. It was neither received nor totally rejected but returned to a committee for a vote in November 1992.[30] In November 1992 it did not receive the required votes to pass. The non-reception of these drafts, each of which restates the prohibition on the ordination of women, may provide added insight into the reception of the prohibition on the ordination of women.

In the rejected first draft of the pastoral, concerns of women are cited:

> The long-standing practice of the church, according to which only men are ordained to the priesthood, has become a source of frustration and even alienation; . . . the gifts of ordained women would do much to strengthen the mission and ministry of the church; . . . can the church proclaim that women and men are equal and deny ordination to women?; . . . some women are offended by the very suggestion that a woman because of her sex cannot represent Christ or image him as a priest; . . . eucharistic celebration has become an occasion of divisiveness, pain and frustration; . . . some women refuse to participate in the liturgy because it is presided over by men only. Concelebrated Masses at times highlight this difficulty; . . . some have left the church to participate in worship led by women; . . . many women find the restriction of ordination to the priesthood to men as arbitrary and counterproductive to the overall good of the church in our time.[31]

In the second draft the bishops responded that the issues cited caused them great pastoral concern. They, nevertheless, reiterate the prohibition[32] that stated that throughout the course of history the church has resolved questions about the permanency of some practice or doctrine by a judgment of its *magisterium*[33] and recommend that the question of admission of women to the diaconal office be submitted to thorough investigation.[34]

It is of particular interest to our study that the bishops are concerned that communion within the Roman Catholic Church be sustained by those who do not peacefully receive the decision to exclude women from the ministerial priesthood. The bishops stated that:

> it is our sincere prayer now and in the future that controversy over the admission of women to the ordained priesthood will not lead Catholics to absent themselves from the sacred liturgy that unites us expressly

30. *Idem.*
31. "Partners," n. 197–201.
32. "One in Christ," n. 115.
33. *Ibid.,* n. 116.
34. *Ibid.,* n. 120.

to Christ and to each other. We pray that disagreement will not cause anyone to take leave of the church, for whom Christ gave his life.[35]

Diverse groups within the church did not receive the drafts of the pastoral on women.[36] For some groups a reason for non-reception of the pastoral was the prohibition of the ordination of women. The Executive Committee of the Leadership Conference of Women Religious stated that

> the draft offers no resolution of the difficulties and repeats the unsatisfactory phrase from *Inter Insigniores,* "the church in fidelity to the example of the Lord does not consider herself authorized to admit women to priestly ordination". . . . This position continues to stand in opposition to all protestations of desire that women be incorporated fully into decision-making roles in the church.[37]

From another position, Women for Faith and Family requested that the bishops drop the pastoral because the committee could not "produce a sound document" that would be acceptable to "intrinsically incompatible" groups of women in the church.[38]

Other reasons for postponing the vote on the pastoral were linked to community and reception. The bishops sought more responses at home and abroad. The Holy See suggested postponement because "consultation with bishops' conferences of other countries on this pastoral letter would be appropriate."[39] At the consultation requested by the Holy See, the five curial officials pointed to the need for more profound anthropology.[40]

The third draft, "Called to be One in Christ," reduced the section on the ministerial priesthood from nine to four paragraphs and restated the prohibition. In the non-reception of this draft in June 1992, bishops acknowledged that the critical issue is that of ordination of women. Most who addressed the issue of ordination acknowledged the need to explain the church teaching more fully and convincingly, but two bishops expressed opposition to or serious reservations about the teaching itself.[41]

35. *Ibid.,* n. 119.

36. See Daniel Pilarczyk, "Vote on Women's Pastoral Delayed," *Origins* 20:16 (1990) 250–251. See also, *The National Catholic Reporter* 27:33, 6–7.

37. LCWR Executive Committee, "Critiquing the Women's Pastoral Draft," *Origins* 20:12 (1990) 186–187.

38. See Paul Likoudis, "Women's Pastoral Postponed Indefinitely by NCCB Committee," *The Wanderer* 123:39, 1.

39. Pilarczyk (n. 36).

40. Vatican Consultation, "Concerns Expressed about U.S. Bishops' Draft Pastoral on Women," *Origins* 21:5 (1991) 74–75.

41. Filteau (n. 28).

Summary of the Catholic Position

We may conclude that there has been both reception and non-reception of the official declaration which prohibits women from the priestly ministry by members of the Roman Catholic Church. There are indications that the prohibition has been received. We know of no Roman Catholic bishop in the United States who has ordained a Roman Catholic woman. Many Roman Catholics, laity and clergy, assent to the prohibition with mind, heart, and will. Others receive the prohibition with their will if not with their heart and mind. It may also be said that the prohibition has not been received. Some Roman Catholic laity and clergy do not give their assent to the prohibition;[42] some promote the ordination of women. Others have left the Roman Catholic Church over the issue, and of these some men and women have sought ordination in the Episcopal Church or in other Christian churches that ordain women. The fact that the prohibition has been both received and not received produces a strain on communion among believers within the Roman Catholic Church. This strain has not yet resulted in either a solution or a schism.

Conclusion

As stated in the previous chapter, neither the 1975 letters of Pope Paul VI to the archbishop of Canterbury, Donald Coggan, concerning the ordination of women to the priesthood nor the October 1976 Declaration of the prohibition were received by the Episcopal Church in the United States or by the other churches within the Anglican communion which have ordained women. Some Episcopalians find the prohibition a reason for discontinuing the search for full communion between the two churches.

It seems evident that leaders in each communion, while taking seriously the opinion of the other, make decisions out of their own experiences and theological positions when they address the issue of women in the ministerial priesthood. The movement in opposite directions on this issue

---

42. On May 30, 1994, Pope John Paul II reiterated in an apostolic letter, *Ordinatio Sacerdotalis,* the teaching that "the church has no authority whatsoever to confer priestly ordination on women." The reason for issuing the letter seemed to be a concern for the non-reception of the prohibition. The Pope states, "at the present time in some places it [the teaching that priestly ordination is to be reserved to men alone] is nonetheless considered still open to debate." A number of bishops of the United States issued statements of reception of the apostolic letter, *Ordinatio Sacerdotalis.* Another issue related to authority and reception raised in the apostolic letter is the terminology that its teaching "is to be definitely held by all the church's faithful." (See "Apostolic Letter on Ordination and Women," "An Overview of the Apostolic Letter," and "Bishops React to *Ordinatio Sacerdotalis,*" *Origins* 24:16 [1994] 49–58.)

is often considered the most serious obstacle to full communion. It is encouraging, however, that Anglican–Roman Catholic relations have sustained such a profound disagreement.

The 1991 ARCIC II report, "Church as Communion," calls Anglicans and Roman Catholics to affirm their real and yet imperfect communion and to recognize the degree of communion that exists between the two churches. Referring to obstacles to full communion, including the ordination of women, ARCIC II states:

> These [remaining obstacles] should encourage Anglicans and Roman Catholics locally to search for further steps by which concrete expressions can be given to this communion which we share.[43]

As agreements are reached on issues that divided our churches in the past, contemporary situations provide an ever greater need for the Anglican and Roman Catholic Churches to apply Gospel values and Christian principles to current challenges.

43. "Church as Communion" (n. 1) n. 58.

14

The Pastoral Provision

Reception and Non-Reception

The "Pastoral Provision" is a case of reception that involves new aspects of ecumenism: the acceptance into the Roman Catholic Church of married and unmarried Episcopal priests who are subsequently ordained as Roman Catholic priests. Though the provision was created in response to a pastoral need (the discomfort felt by some clergy with the ordination of women to the priesthood and episcopate in some churches of the Anglican communion), the effect of the provision has been to create suspicion in the minds of some Episcopalians concerning the intentions of the Roman Catholic Church in regard to ecumenism and to slow ecumenical progress among Episcopalians and Roman Catholics.

The Background of the Pastoral Provision

In 1977 several groups of Episcopal priests, as well as individuals, both clergy and lay, initiated appeals to various Roman Catholic bishops. There were two types of requests to the bishops: individual married Episcopal priests sought full communion with the Roman See and the possibility of serving as married priests in Latin rite dioceses; other priests, married and celibate, sought full communion with the Roman See with the ability to function as priests for communities of former Episcopalians while maintaining some liturgical aspects of their Anglican heritage.

During the previous ten years these Anglo-Catholic Episcopalians in the United States had become increasingly concerned about what they saw as "a breakdown in the doctrinal and moral integrity of their church."[1] Above all they pointed to the 1976 vote to ordain women to the priesthood as a cause for concern. The ordination of women caused these groups to despair of any eventual Anglican reunion with the Roman See.

1. Bernard F. Law, "Progress Report on the Pastoral Provision" (February 1985, A report distributed to the National Conference of Catholic Bishops) 1.

In August 1980 the Congregation for the Doctrine of the Faith announced that a positive decision on these requests had been taken by Pope John Paul II. The Roman Congregation announced outlines for a "Pastoral Provision" for former Episcopal priests and lay people; this was originally to be limited to the United States. In February 1981 Bishop Bernard Law was appointed by the CDF to function as its ecclesiastical delegate in this matter in the United States, and in May 1981 the National Conference of Catholic Bishops provided funds to cover support and office costs for a full-time assistant to the delegate. This assistant was the Reverend James Parker, a married former Episcopal priest who had been for a number of years North American provincial vicar of the Society of the Holy Cross and the principal leader in the initial Episcopal requests to the Roman See.

By January 1985 rescripts, formal documents of approval, had been issued to provide for the ordination of twenty-five former Episcopal priests. Of these twenty-three were married. Ten years after the first petition was made, the forty-second married Episcopal priest was ordained to the Roman Catholic priesthood by Cardinal John O'Connor of New York in May 1989. The small number of Episcopal clergy responding to the Vatican invitation was a disappointment to those who had initiated the provision from within the Episcopal Church and to its backers in Rome.[2]

While the majority of petitioners presented themselves to Rome as individuals, some wished to be received with groups of laypersons. The provision included the possibility of erecting these congregations into "personal parishes" to allow for the preservation of certain elements of their Anglican heritage. The former Episcopal rector would be ordained to serve as the Roman Catholic pastor. The provision allowed that certain liturgical usages of the Book of Common Prayer be retained in these Roman parishes. In 1984 an interim "Anglican-use" liturgy was approved by the Roman See for use in these parishes.

The first of these Anglican-use personal parishes was erected in San Antonio by a decree of the local bishop in August 1983. Others are in Las Vegas, Austin, Houston, and Columbia, South Carolina. By 1990 a sixth Anglican-use parish was getting under way in the Atlanta Archdiocese.

A New Departure

The Pastoral Provision thus went beyond the phenomenon of married Roman Catholic clergy. What was a true departure was the introduc-

2. Joseph H. Fichter, *The Pastoral Provisions—Married Catholic Priests* (Kansas City: Sheed and Ward, 1989) 1.

tion of congregations of former Anglicans who would continue their liturgical, sacramental, and ritual traditions within the Roman Catholic Church. The parishes are the real ecumenical problem with the Pastoral Provision, for while the married priests could be absorbed and will eventually die out, the parishes are a continuing monument to the Anglican tradition of Catholicism within the Roman Catholic Church. In the process there has been the transfer of some Anglican liturgical and ritual usage into the Roman Catholic Church. On the positive side, this situation might be taken to illustrate the recognition by Vatican Council II that "Catholic traditions and institutions continue to exist"[3] within the Anglican communion. But the negative side is summarized by Joseph H. Fichter, a sociologist, in this way:

> One gets the impression that at the hierarchical level of both Churches these Anglican-usage parishes are accepted in an embarrassed silence. The Catholic authorities insist that they are not ecumenical; the Episcopal authorities are afraid that they may become ecumenical.[4]

The whole issue raises the specter of the Eastern rites that have caused some problems for the Roman Catholic Church in the nineteenth and twentieth centuries. Eastern Catholic churches, sometimes referred to as uniate, are members of the communion of the Roman Catholic Church. As autonomous churches they express or live the Christian faith through their own theology, spirituality, liturgy, and canon law. Some of the Eastern Catholic churches have felt that the terms of their union with Rome have not been fully respected over the years, and that they have occasionally been treated as second-class citizens who form a part of a "colonial office" of the Vatican.

The Roman Catholic View

When Rome first opened the opportunity for married Episcopal priests to transfer to the Roman Catholic Church in 1980, the president of the National Conference of Catholic Bishops, Archbishop John Quinn, said that this was not meant to stall the Anglican–Roman Catholic ecumenical process, and in 1982 the apostolic delegate for the Pastoral Provision, Bishop Bernard Law, stated that this procedure did not mean a "diminution of commitment to the ecumenical movement."[5] In a survey of Roman Catholic priests ordained in the last ten years, 66 percent of diocesan priests

3. *Ibid.,* 26.
4. *Ibid.,* 4.
5. See *ibid.,* 15.

and 68 percent of religious priests expressed a willingness to accept married and unmarried former Episcopal priests as colleagues in the Roman Catholic priesthood.

But concern about the ecumenical impact of the Provision has been clearly voiced by officials and publications of the Roman Catholic Church. In a conversation in January 1985, a high Vatican official made the following points:

> 1. that the Pastoral Provision is a very serious ecumenical matter which had not been discussed in advance and in detail with the Vatican Secretariat for Christian Unity.

> 2. that the Pastoral Provision means that there are two levels of ecumenical encounter going on in the Roman Catholic Church: one official, conducted by the Pontifical Council for Christian Unity, and one unofficial, conducted by the Congregation for the Doctrine of the Faith. This seems in keeping with the style of Pope John Paul II who likes to carry on several levels of policy on an issue at once.[6]

The Roman Catholic journal *Worship* has been severely critical of the liturgical and ecumenical implications of the provision. Here is an excerpt from a May 1985 editorial in *Worship* on the Anglican-use liturgy for the Pastoral Provision parishes:

> The result, especially in the case of Rite I of the Holy Eucharist, is quite hybrid: traditional Book of Common Prayer for the liturgy of the word and the precommunion and postcommunion prayers; prayers for the presentation of the gifts, including the proper prayer over the gifts, from the 1970 Roman Missal according to the ICEL translation; traditional Book of Common Prayer preface; and the Roman Canon as translated by Miles Coverdale. This, it seems to me, is more conducive to schizophrenia than to a secure sense of identity. . . . The *Book of Divine Worship* is intended exclusively for the use of the priests and laity of the "Pastoral Provision". . . . It seems unlikely that anyone else would be tempted to use it.[7]

Here we see that the Vatican decision to mix a traditional Anglican liturgy with the Roman Canon is a factor that stands in the way of reception and builds barriers between the churches. For Anglicans this suggests a rejection of the orthodoxy of the Anglican Eucharistic prayer.

Views in the Episcopal Church

While the Roman Catholic Church's attitude toward the provision may be characterized as divided, since some have received the new departure

6. Conversation of a Vatican official on January 3, 1985.
7. "Anglican Use Liturgy," *Worship* 59 (May 1985) 265.

and others have rejected it, the attitude in the Episcopal Church has grown increasingly critical and now may be characterized as solidly negative. Not only can the case be made that the provision has not been received in the Episcopal Church, but there has been a growing institutional position that the provision signals a half-hearted Roman commitment to ecumenism despite protestations to the contrary. Thus we have here an example of a new development in one church not being "received" by the other partner and of this lack of reception creating imbalance and new barriers. This case can be made by demonstrating an increasing groundswell of negative reaction in the Episcopal Church which reached a climax in several public protests and warnings issued by the Episcopal Church to the Roman Catholic Church.

By 1985 voices were being publicly raised in the Episcopal Church outlining the ecumenical consequences of the Pastoral Provision. That year Robert Terwilliger, suffragan bishop of Dallas, found that there is an "obvious tension between those proposals and the ecumenical dialogue going on between our Church and the Roman Catholic Church." J. Robert Wright, theological consultant to the Episcopal Church's ecumenical office, felt that this high-level policy of the Vatican "must raise questions of the Roman Church's official ecumenical sincerity, integrity and sensitivity in the eyes not only of Anglicans but also of other churches." The bishop of the diocese of Massachusetts, John Coburn, was disturbed that in this action Rome once again demonstrated and reinforced a public and official rejection of the validity of Episcopal ordinations. He predicted that "there will be no future of institutional cooperation of any great significance until this is dealt with again."[8]

Following such statements the Episcopal Church began to suggest in various ways its lack of reception of the Pastoral Provision and its assessment of the damage that was being done to the ecumenical movement. These reactions came in four stages:

1. *Statement of the Ecumenical Officer of the Episcopal Church.* In a letter intended to be shared with officials at the Vatican, the Ecumenical Officer wrote on June 14, 1985:

> In pluralistic America we are accustomed to Christians moving from church to church. It is quite a different matter for one church to organize parishes and institute liturgy taken from another church— all to satisfy the individual wishes of a very few people who have moved. Comments in my hearing from individual Episcopalians, including some bishops, about the parishes and proposed Anglican rite have been uniformly negative. This is simply a fact.[9]

8. On these reactions, see Fichter, 15, 24.
9. Letter of Ecumenical Officer to the Right Reverend Theodore Eastman and the Reverend Christopher Hill, June 14, 1985.

2. *Statement of the Standing Liturgical Commission.* In 1986 the Standing Liturgical Commission of the Episcopal Church sent a memorandum to the Standing Commission on Ecumenical Relations concerning the Pastoral Provision. Concerns expressed to the commission by both Anglican and Roman Catholic liturgists about the liturgical integrity of these "hybrid rites" as well as their possible permanency resulted in the official request that lines of communication be opened to Rome protesting the Pastoral Provision.[10]

3. *Statement of ARC-USA.* As a result of these concerns, the Episcopal Church members of ARC-USA asked that body to pass a resolution of warning of the potential damage that could result from the Pastoral Provision. That warning included the following statements:

> Members of ARC-USA were particularly concerned about the corporate dimension of the provision (admission of parishes), the use and modification of Anglican formulations for Liturgy, provision for absolute reordination and lack of provision for consultation. . . . We recommend that the ecumenical implications concerning the transfer of obedience of corporate communities be carefully examined.[11]

4. *Action of the Standing Commission on Ecumenical Relations.* In compliance with the directions of the Ecumenical Commission of the Episcopal Church, three members of the commission, Bishops E. W. Jones, R. F. Grein, and H. W. Shipps, met with Cardinal Bernard Law and Bishop William H. Keeler in July 1986 to officially express Episcopal Church concerns about the Pastoral Provision. The subject of the meeting involved the concerns about the Pastoral Provision expressed at the February 1986 meeting of the commission. Discussion occurred on the need for consultation at the diocesan level concerning priests of either church entering the ministerial priesthood of the other church. The Roman Catholic Church on this occasion regretted that release of information on the Pastoral Provision had not occurred much earlier in the process.[12]

Conclusions

The case of the Pastoral Provision shows that though the aspiration for Christian unity between Anglicans and Roman Catholics is still strong the churches are not standing still: theology and style of leadership continue to evolve within the two churches, sometimes creating fresh barriers and new obstacles. The old procedures of the ecumenical movement, forged in the different atmosphere of the 1960s and 1970s, have been in-

10. Minutes of the Standing Liturgical Commission of the Episcopal Church, January 1986, 7.

11. Memorandum of ARC-USA to the Most Reverend William Keeler, Chair of NCCB/BCEIA, October 15, 1985.

12. Memorandum of the Right Reverend H. W. Shipps to the Standing Commission on Ecumenical Relations of the Episcopal Church on Meeting with Cardinal Law, July 15, 1986.

adequate to meet the challenge of these new forms of negative reception. The result is a growing suspicion and hostility which is leading to the conclusion that the two churches are in a state of "broken dialogue." Unless the churches face seriously the responsibility for developing new mechanisms of dialogue that can handle non-reception, years of progress could be thrown away. Unless quickly resolved, the growing impact of this example of non-reception—the Pastoral Provision—has the potential for leaving the ecumenical movement and the Christian churches even more sadly divided. We trust that the lessons learned from this experience in the United States will now be applied to the fluid situation of Anglican–Roman Catholic relations in Britain now, in Australia, and other parts of the globe.

RECEPTION
AND
COMMUNITY

15

Receiving the Vision

The Spirit at Work

Dealing with the subject of reception as a process in the Roman Catholic Church, Avery Dulles says that reception "belongs, or should belong, to the very kernel of any sound Christian theology" for "theology is a methodical reflection on faith, and faith is something that must be received."[1] In a report by the House of Bishops of the Church of England we read:

> The last twenty years have seen the recovery of the concept of reception. Attention has been given to the question how conciliar statements were received in the life of the early Church. And reception has come to the centre of the ecumenical discussion in relation to the way in which the fruits of ecumenical dialogues, like the Lima Text and *The Final Report* of ARCIC, are received in the life of the Churches. . . . Reception is not passive obedience to conciliar statements but a living process in which church leaders, together with the faithful, respond and receive into their lives the insights of a council. The process is an open one . . . if, in the course of time, the Church as a whole receives a conciliar decision, this would be an additional or final sign that it may be judged to be in accordance with God's will for the Church.[2]

Our spiritual understanding of reception needs a theological rationale or underpinning for the churches as they undertake the long pilgrimage to reestablish visible credible Christian unity. As Dulles noted, "without reception there could be no authentic Christianity."[3] Such a statement

---

1. Avery Dulles, "The Reception Process in the Roman Catholic Church." Paper delivered to the Twenty-second International Seminar at Strasbourg (July 2, 1988).
2. *The Ordination of Women to the Priesthood: A Second Report by the House of Bishops of the General Synod of the Church of England* (GS 829) 106–107. Available from the Church House, Great Smith Street, London SW1P 3NZ, United Kingdom.
3. Dulles (n. 1).

is simply a way of saying that the notion of reception has its foundation in faith, i.e., the reception of God's revealed word and work through the church as sacrament and sign of God's mysterious relationship with us in Christ. Reception is related both to the Scriptures and Tradition. We have received Jesus Christ (Col 2:6) and his Gospel (1 Cor 15:1; Gal 1:9-12) and are responsible for "handing on" what we have received (1 Cor 11:33). Paul reminds Timothy of this obligation (2 Tim 2:2). As a community of faith the church receives and appropriates apostolic faith—a faith to be received and communicated. Reception is the very life of the Church—a receiving and a giving.

The notion of reception is used in two ways. There is what may we call a classical usage and an ecumenical usage. One usage cannot be entirely divorced from the other, though much of contemporary usage is for ecumenical purposes.

The Classical View of Reception

This view has a rather explicit scriptural base in Acts 15, which has to be read with care. While it deals with decision-making on the part of Peter and James in the apostolic hierarchy, this is not to be taken as an emphasis exclusively on institutional leadership. The church does not view reception as coming down from above through a chain of command, requiring only passive obedience and conformity. The report of the bishops of the Church of England just quoted is clear on that matter. Reception is in fact an act of discernment throughout the whole church. The decisions of that first ecumenical council of Jerusalem were reached by "the apostles and the elders, with the whole Church." Reception in this classical sense presupposed a united church which strengthened its bonds of communion and interpreted its doctrine through a representative council. Doctrine is to be received by the church as a whole when it is seen to be in continuity with its received tradition. This continuity involves the historical reality of the church's life in a current situation. Thus there has to be emphasis on dialogue which reveals such continuity between past and present. Dialogue is not always easy, and much less does it lead to immediate solutions. Much dialogue is necessary at times, and reception is more often than not a long process, sometimes taking many years or decades. The process is necessarily time-consuming because it is not the isolated activity of church leaders in conference. Discernment must be both dialogical and experiential, and these two elements must influence and assist one another if there is to be real discernment under the grace of the Holy Spirit. In the end of the discernment-reception process, the whole Church must be able to say: "For it has seemed good to the Holy Spirit and to us to impose on you no further burden than these essentials. . . ."

When we speak about the "faith of the Church," we are not thinking only of creedal or theological statements of doctrine. We have to take into account the actual faith of believers, i.e., their experience in faith. Creeds and dogmas are indispensable to set the boundaries of formal belief, to maintain essential truth, to guard against false interpretations, but reception is no less important because it is a process "by which the magisterial and other pronouncements of authorities and theologians interpret the authoritative declarations of the Church in a manner which resonates with the actual faith of Christians and does not undermine the doctrinally defined authority of various officeholders in the Church."[4]

Scripture itself illustrates the classical notion of reception by the church. The formation of the scriptural canon is the end of a process in which certain writings were received through their actual "use in Christian communities and whose content was already held to be apostolic" in such a way that these writings "came to be confirmed and adopted as authoritative for the Church."[5] Thomas Ryan, following the lead of Ulrich Kuhn, notes "a certain narrowness in dealing with the idea of reception in the ancient Church compared with its breadth in the New Testament."[6] He expands this observation when he says:

> In the first place, attention has been concentrated, particularly in the pre-Constantinian period (before 310), on decisions made by local or regional synods which were made known to other churches by means of synodal letters, and accepted by these churches. Underlying this was the realization that a particular church is only authentically the Church if it lives in fellowship with other churches. In the second place, attention has been focused on decisions made by the imperial councils since Constantine and the reception process that began only when the council ended. In both these processes, the role of formal juridical acts by church authorities is a relatively subordinate one of confirmation and completion. Since reception is a spiritual and theological process whereby decisions taken in the Church are accepted . . . the only adequate way of understanding it is to reinsert it in the wider New Testament framework of the spiritual event of transmission and acceptance—a fundamental process for the life of Christians and the Church.[7]

4. Myroslaw Tataryn, "Karl Rahner and the Nature of Reception," *One in Christ* 25 (1989) 78.

5. Thomas Ryan, "Reception: Unpacking the New Holy Word," *Ecumenism* 82 (1983) 28.

6. *Idem.* See Ulrich Kuhn, "Reception: An Imperative and an Opportunity," in *Ecumenical Perspectives on Baptism, Ministry and Eucharist* (Geneva: World Council of Churches, 1983); E. Sullivan, "Reception: Factor and Moment in Ecumenism," *Ecumenical Trends* 15:7 (July–August 1986) 105–110, with Roman Catholic, Protestant, and Evangelical responses following.

7. Ryan, 28.

If we are to deal with reception in its ecumenical usage, we have to appreciate different theological approaches to its classical usage. Some theologians, like Nikos Nissiotis, emphasize the role of councils, while others, like Karl Rahner, cast reception in the wider mold suggested by Ulrich Kuhn. Another way of expressing reception is in terms of Scripture and tradition. When we accept Scripture and tradition as the single source of Christian revelation we are better able to understand why there cannot be a complete disjunction between the classical and ecumenical functions of reception. If we tie reception too tightly to the decision-making process of church councils and the statements of the early Fathers of the church, we are forced to agree with Nissiotis that the classical view differs significantly from the ecumenical view inasmuch as the latter has to take into account the historic divisions of the churches.[8] Both approaches are legitimate and both entail consequences for the ecumenical movement. Nissiotis would, of course, grant that biblical factors and the praxis of ancient churches prior to the schisms of the eleventh and sixteenth centuries "point to the common origins and purposes of these two kinds of reception." Yet for him "these councils mediate the operation of the Holy Spirit (Acts 15:8) upon those gathered at the same place with one accord . . . and those who receive conciliar decisions, i.e., the local churches as parts of the Church universal. It is," he says, "precisely this presupposition . . . which has been shaken in modern times by the schismatic church situation."[9] Rahner, on the other hand, did not emphasize the schismatic condition of the churches. He saw our present differences and divisions as "the product of historical events whose contemporary theological significance no longer necessitates the maintenance of a state of schism."[10] Rahner began with the basic unity of faith rather than with the presupposition of a basic disunity. Whereas the classical view of reception sustained visible unity, the ecumenical view reestablishes that visible unity. Ecumenical reception witnesses to what is fundamental in Christian experience though presently lived out in a plurality of historically divided churches. Yet even this way of expressing the two views of reception proves inadequate if we remember that church councils were usually convened when church unity was threatened, and such councils were held to reestablish visible unity.

This is not idle speculation. The wider view of classical reception highlights the dynamic relationship between Scripture and tradition. This view

8. See Nikos Nissiotis, "The Meaning of Reception in Relation to the Results of Ecumenical Dialogue on the Basis of Faith and Order Document 'Baptism, Eucharist, and Ministry,' " *The Greek Orthodox Review* 30:2 (Summer 1985) 151.

9. *Ibid.*, 153.

10. Tataryn (n. 4) 81. I am indebted to this treatment of Karl Rahner's approach to reception.

also reminds ecumenically spirited Christians that a high degree of continuity has been ensured by the Holy Spirit even in periods of notable divisions, differences, and deviations in doctrine and practice. This wider view takes the present ecumenical age of the church to be a time to reestablish an older, more visible unity among Christian churches. This wider view of reception promises us a new opportunity to discover a richer, fuller and perhaps unprecedented expression of the catholic character of the church. Such unity will be a unity in diversity, organic, a truly conciliar fellowship wherein churches are united in true communion without being absorbed, in such a way that legitimate gifts and traditions are fully respected.

The Ecumenical View of Reception

The ecumenical usage shares important aspects of reception with the older classical view. We must remember, however, that it is a process, that it takes time. Given the history of our divisions, ecumenical reception takes a lot of time. This is so because a long process of maturation is needed to incorporate new elements of doctrinal development and liturgy, along with discipline and spirituality, into new structures of church unity. There must be time to come to terms and to justify the practices of particular churches in the light of apostolic faith as it is understood in particular types of churches. Only seven councils in the early church came to be recognized as ecumenical councils. In our day separated churches are being asked to respond to the Lima Document by considering how faithful it is to their understanding of their churches as reflections of the apostolic faith in the areas of baptism, Eucharist, and ministry. Roman Catholics are still receiving the renewed life engendered by Vatican Council II.[11] Reception may involve doctrine or specific decisions on church discipline expressed in canon law and in church ordinances drawn up for a particular time or situation. In time doctrine develops, while disciplinary laws and ordinances may quietly cease to be effective or practical. Ordinances may be negated or modified once they have served their purpose in relation to essential Christian doctrine.

In our time reception is ultimately related to theological dialogue over church-dividing and church-uniting issues. Thus what we call "faith and order" issues remain at the center of the ecumenical movement. In 1963 the Faith and Order Conference of the World Council of Churches held in Montreal decided that the best way to make progress in ecumenical dialogue was to return to the theological sources prior to the schisms of the

11. See Gabriel Daly, "How Well has Vatican II Been Received," *Doctrine and Life* 39 (1989) 412–420.

eleventh and sixteenth centuries, to a time when significant areas of visible unity existed in the life and doctrine of the church as a communion of churches. This helped the ecumenical movement greatly, and not least Anglicans and Roman Catholics as evidenced by the work of ARCIC I. Dialogue is a key to reception since it is not an academic exercise for theologians but involves the whole church. Dialogue is intended to express Christian truths to be fed into the daily life of the churches as they live and work together. Dialogue does not establish truth, however, but bears witness to it.

Reception is the work of the Spirit in the life of the church, and dialogue along with other forms of Christian interaction is the Spirit leading us to a richer grasp of truth. This work is manifested in an effort to understand, to encourage, to edify, and to ensure a growing convergence in doctrine and life among the churches. From time to time substantial agreement is reached. To appreciate ecumenical reception and to keep our churches mutually open to receiving gifts and graces from one another, the work of the Holy Spirit must be kept at the center of "faith and order" work. The doctrine of the Spirit's activity in the Body of Christ cannot be treated as a concession to piety. The Holy Spirit has led the Christian churches to discover a variety of spiritual goods during the centuries of separation. A rich heritage of spiritual goods developed as denominations went their separate ways. But the gifts and graces developed in the Spirit are meant to be shared in the whole church; the gifts of the Spirit are for the whole church. Whatever model of church unity may be favored by particular churches, the church as a communion of communions stands for the truth that we are called to receive and share what the Spirit gives. Nissiotis comments that where we anticipate some form of structural unity, reception appears "in a new meaning, a new form and praxis, as an ecclesial category of paramount importance for all the churches struggling for the renewal of their life."[12] Any theological rationale must take into account two dimensions of reception. First, one must receive what God has done and is doing in the denominational life of one's own church. Second, one has to acknowledge and receive what God has done and is doing in the life of other churches.

Recognition and Reception

Recognition is decisive in the reception process since it frees us "from our instinctive fear of the other as stranger and our anxious concern for our own identity."[13] In an important footnote of the common statement

12. Nissiotis, 155.

13. *Facing Unity*. A common statement by the Roman Catholic/Lutheran Joint Commission, Geneva (Lutheran World Federation, 1985) 22.

issued by the International Joint Commission of Lutherans and Roman Catholics, *Facing Unity,* the relationship between recognition and reception is spelled out:

> The term "reception" is often used with regard to accepting specific statements or documents, but here we intend both terms, "reception" and "recognition," to be designators of interchurch relations and actions: "Recognition" means basically a theological and spiritual affirmation of the other church in its special emphases, which confers on this church as a whole or an individual elements of its belief, life, or structure legitimacy and authenticity. "Reception" means basically a theological and spiritual affirmation of the other church as a whole or in individual elements of its belief, life or structure which accepts and appropriates the special emphasis of the other church either as its own or as contributions (in the sense of correction or complement).[14]

Here we have a clear statement that there can be no reception apart from a recognition of the legitimacy and authenticity of the other church here and now. Recognition and reception are complementary. Reception is the end product for it "emphasizes more strongly the special character of the other as containing elements to be adopted and integrated into a church's own life and thinking and into its fellowship with the other church."[15]

If these factors of recognition and reception apply to churches of the ecumenical movement, they certainly apply to the way in which ecumenical documents are to be read. Earlier we mentioned the need for ecumenical formation in the spiritual reading of such texts as *Facing Unity, The Final Report,* and the Lima Document. This means that ecumenists must be concerned about the way such texts reach the general membership of the churches, assuming they have some awareness of the church as a community, a living organism animated by the Holy Spirit. Reception is possible where the image of the church as the body of Christ has been developed and the church is seen to be composed of diverse functions and gifts, and that our churches are linked to one another in Christ for the sharing of gifts for the common good of Christian life, witness, and mission.

The Intrinsic Authority of Ecumenical Texts

Where there is no theological understanding of ecumenism, such texts as the Lima Document, *The Final Report,* and *Facing Unity* are often dismissed as products of pragmatic bargaining among theologians and ec-

14. *Idem.*
15. *Ibid.,* 24.

clesiastics and not seen as the fruit of discernment in the Spirit. It is true that these texts take their authority from those who produce them, but they are intended for the churches as a whole for further discernment. They bear witness to the unity of faith we wish to express as Christians to the extent that they are received by the churches. Little has been said about the intrinsic authority of such texts for the churches to which they are directed for response and action. Each time such texts are put forward a question is addressed to the churches: What does it mean to the church, living in obedience to God's will? Because ecumenism is a movement of the Holy Spirit, these texts take their value from a growing convergence of life and apostolic faith among churches. Jean Tillard speaks of a crucial relationship between bilateral dialogues and the church's tradition in the concrete and specific situation of human history. The dialogue takes as its point of departure matters of doctrine held in common. Along the way those involved may discover definite divergencies which may lead the churches involved to an act of renewed faith which opens their present denominational horizon to a more universal, truly ecumenical horizon.[16]

The way they are produced also lends authority and integrity to ecumenical documents. Even as the communion of our churches is imperfect, so is their ability to act and speak together. In the present ecumenical context the churches tend toward full communion through dialogue and other ecumenical activities. Dialogue is an effective exercise by which the churches endeavor to form a common conscience and speak the truth together in love. Ecumenical documents reflect this conciliar communion, however imperfectly it is presently expressed. The effort to speak and act together manifests a genuine desire for full communion by whatever model of church unity this is envisaged. Documents like ARCIC I's *The Final Report* ask some response from their constituent churches. The Lima Document is remarkable in itself because it gave rise to the Lima Liturgy which allows some churches to celebrate the Eucharist together. This reflects something of the intrinsic value of the text. Those able to celebrate the Lima Liturgy have another avenue to express the growing unity of the churches and to make a statement of common faith according to the revered rule that prayer reflects the faith of the Church, *lex orandi lex credendi.*

16. See the following articles in the *Journal of Ecumenical Studies*: Edward Kilmartin, "Reception in History: An Ecclesiological Phenomenon and its Significance" *JES*: 21, 1 (1984) 34–54; Jean Tillard, "The Ecclesiological Implications of Bilateral Dialogue," *JES* 23:3 (1986) 412–423; Michael Kinnamon, "Bilaterals and the Uniting and United Churches, *JES* 23:3 (1986) 377–385; Kortright Davis, "Bilateral Dialogue and Contextualizations," *JES* 23:3 (1986) 386–399; John Ford, "Bilateral Conversations and Denominational Horizons," *JES* 23:3 (1986) 518–528.

Response and Reception

William Rusch speaks of response as "an early step in the process that is reception."[17] Ecumenical documents are looking for some response from the churches on whose behalf they have been written. They ask for some response as a precondition for reception or non-reception, as the case may be. The response is a way of determining whether the agreements and convergencies reached conform to a given church's understanding of apostolic faith. The results of dialogue ought not be judged by their conformity to particular denominational theology and practice, but by some essential understanding and conviction of the Christian faith throughout the ages. Of course, church authorities have to honor this process. They cannot sit in judgment on a document as if they are standing apart from and outside the result of ecumenical dialogue. They ought to seek ways of involving the general membership of their respective churches in making such a response. Reception is a delicate web of theological competence and spiritual discernment, always coupled with a desire to be faithful to Christ in his will for the unity of his disciples. Without an official response enthusiasm at the parish or congregational level for such agreed statements is unlikely. An official response, and a studied response from the members of the churches in general, are needed if the discernment of reception or non-reception is to work.

The conclusions of a dialogue and the response to a document are not a commitment to approve all that appears there. Response is not reception and reception implies the possibility of non-reception. The Lima Document did not ask for reception but for a response according to the following norms:

> 1) To what extent can your church recognize in this text the faith of the Church through the ages;
>
> 2) What consequences can your church draw from this text for its relations and dialogues with other churches, particularly with those churches which also recognize the text as an expression of apostolic faith;
>
> 3) What guidance can your church take from this text for its worship, its educational, ethical, and spiritual life and witness.[18]

17. William Rusch, *Reception: An Ecumenical Opportunity* (Philadelphia: Fortress Press, 1988) 28.

18. *Baptism, Eucharist and Ministry* (Geneva: World Council of Churches, 1982) x. Over one hundred theologians met in Lima, Peru, in January 1982, and recommended unanimously to transmit this agreed statement—the Lima text—for the common study and official response of the churches.

While such documents prompt us to think in terms of reception or non-reception, we must remember that all such documents and agreements are ways of allowing the churches to prepare themselves to receive anew the one apostolic faith in its fullness for a new stage of church unity. The renewed reception of apostolic faith is what ecumenism with its dialogue is all about.

The Reception of the Principles

Over and above the norms that enable churches to make some response to ecumenical findings, there are principles which govern the whole ecumenical movement and hence are normative for the reading and study of ecumenical documents such as the Lima Document, *The Final Report,* and *Facing Unity*. These following principles are basic to the reception process:

1) Unity includes legitimate diversity. Diversity is not something to be tolerated but an integral part of the mystery of Christ and the church. The richness of the church's catholic character and witness is that the Church is for all people of all time.

2) The Lund Principle is a determination on the part of the churches to act together in all matters except those in which deep differences of conviction compel them to act separately.

3) The church must always be ready for reformation. In every age the church must be willing to review and reexamine its fidelity to the Gospel and to the gifts bestowed by the Holy Spirit for its life and mission.

4) Doctrine develops. In preaching the Gospel in every age and to every nation the Church grows in its understanding of the Gospel and of the richness of God's revelation in Christ. Thence it expresses the Gospel and the revelation in new and different ways.

5) The hierarchy of truths is a comparison of various teachings in historically separated churches in relation to the foundational teachings of the Christian faith. These doctrines, developed in one or more churches, are to be received by other churches as legitimate expressions of growth in the faith experience of those churches as they explored the central mysteries of the Trinity and incarnation.

6) To be real, ecumenism must be local. This principle deserves further comment and needs to be expanded.

Local Ecumenism

Any theological rationale must be concerned with the taking of ecumenism into the bloodstream of the church's life. Whether it takes place on a "slow drip" or by direct transfusion, ecumenism is meant to enter the life of our parishes and congregations. That is what local means. Local may also refer to diocesan or regional church structures, but whatever meaning we assign to local ecumenism it is the lived experience of Christians in a given place. This experience must be marked by openness and a readiness to respond to what the Spirit is saying to the churches through the ecumenical movement.

Not all Christians experience the seemingly insurmountable difficulties encountered by theologians and church leaders. While members of churches study the results of theological dialogue and rejoice in the occasional association of church leaders, theologians and church leaders need to monitor the local experience of parishes and congregations. Christian experience, or what we have referred to as the *sensus fidelium,* the instinct for right faith, often enjoys a high degree of development among the lay leaders of our churches. This cannot be written off as excessive enthusiasm. It is often an experience of faith and as such must be respected and listened to. Both theologians and church leaders ought to listen to what the Holy Spirit is saying to them in the daily experience of Christians growing together and sharing the life of one another's churches. The experience of inter-church marriage and family is one significant instance of such experience. However, speaking more generally we can summarize the mutuality implicit in the reception process by saying that what is needed is a healthy interaction of podium, pulpit and pew. The whole church is both a listening, learning, and teaching church. Perhaps this is what Joseph Ratzinger meant when he said:

> Just as the local Church is not just the lowest shading of the universal Church, but rather the immediate and concrete realization of the Church itself, local ecumenism is not just an executing organ of centralized, top-level ecumenism, but rather an original form of ecumenism and an independent starting point for theological insights. This conclusion forces itself upon us with increasing insistence.[19]

Any theological task must be undertaken as a gift as well as a task. Theology is a gift of grace, not an exercise in pure reason. It is a service for the Church as a community of faith and presumes a deep faith. The various fruits of dialogue, and the documents which embody them, are remarkable and must be taken seriously by church leaders, pastors and laity. If they are not received in the right spirit, they cannot break the extreme introversion of our denominations. We need a spirit of biblical *metanoia*, a radical spirit of repentance, if the reception of the ecumeni-

19. Joseph Ratzinger, "Ecumenism on the Local Level," *Information Service of the Secretariat for Promoting Christian Unity* 20, II (April 1973). This secretariat is presently known as the Pontifical Council for Promoting Christian Unity.

cal movement is to happen. It is precisely at this point that local ecumenism must be respected and put into practice. This is where the *sensus fidelium* or *sensus fidei,* the understanding that ecumenism is a vital exercise of faith, becomes operative.

For this reason it may prove helpful to make some general suggestions which could become operative in a more specific way in the life of local churches in order to further the process of ecumenical reception:

> 1) The local church is to be built up as a Christian community, not operated exclusively as an institution.

> 2) Christian congregations need to be kept in touch with the ecumenical movement, that is they must be aware that Christians are growing into unity by stages.

> 3) Pastors ought to create core communities engaged in joint action and study to address ethical, social and spiritual issues in union with other Christian churches and communities.

> 4) Doctrinal differences must be faced honestly while Christians are helped to be hopeful for the future offered them in the ecumenical movement.

> 5) A new tolerance for the diversity we experience and practice in one another's churches needs to be encouraged and such diversity explained.

> 6) Various forms of covenanting between local churches are to be encouraged when and where the relationship between churches has reached sufficient maturity. Covenanting is to be understood as a solemn pledge to God and to each another to pursue specific lines of action which enable churches to enter a deeper ecclesial relationship with one another in order to make more visible and real the ecumenical vision of one united church "that the world may believe."

Conclusion

We have tried to present an overview of what reception means and how it functions in the spiritual-theological dynamic of the ecumenical movement. Our immediate interest is the dialogue and developing relationship between the Roman Catholic and Anglican communions. The dialogue is built on a commitment to seek full communion. The EDEO/NADEO Standing Committee looked at several definitions and descriptions of reception prior to producing this book and they have guided us in our work. We were aware that in this context reception means more than accepting dialogical statements and texts. We were aware that it had to mean a new measure of recognition of one another as churches having a special relationship. Our two churches feel it appropriate to claim some elements of belief and practice found in one another as gifts of the Spirit for the life and structure of each church. Nonetheless, we are aware that the reception process begun in our two churches is at a very early stage. We have yet to take the "findings" of ARCIC I into our churches in such a way that we truly become "sister churches" living in conformity with apostolic tradition, that is, in full communion, respecting the diversity of liturgy and discipline, while remaining free to share both the unity and diversity of liturgy, discipline, and spirituality. Reception must finally mean the assimilation of gifts and graces from one another and their integration into the particular lives of our communions. We have been deeply aware that much of our shared future has yet to be spelled out and clarified. As is abundantly evident from our work, there are a number of serious obstacles to be cleared from the path to our unity as Anglicans and Roman Catholics.

Our committee concludes its work and review of the reception factor in our search for full communion with its own definition:

> Reception is a process by which, under the guidance of the Holy Spirit, Anglicans and Roman Catholics at every level of church life discern in one another's churches elements of praxis, spirituality, doctrine and discipline—in whole or in part—which are authentic expressions of the gospel and apostolic faith. By this mutual discernment we hope to be brought into full visible unity.

Ecumenical Glossary

Apostolic Succession. This is the belief that the church's ordained ministry derives from the apostles by a continuous succession of bishops who, in turn, uphold the apostolic faith. In an earlier period some Roman Catholic scholars questioned whether the historic succession of laying on of hands was broken at the consecration of Matthew Parker as archbishop of Canterbury in 1559. In recent years attention has focused rather on whether the new ordinal (1550) of Edward VI was defective in its form and intention; for example, whether Anglican priests were ordained to a sacrificing priesthood.

ARCIC I. This was the Anglican–Roman Catholic International Commission, established by Pope Paul VI and the then archbishop of Canterbury, the Most Reverend Michael Ramsey. The first meeting was at Windsor Castle from January 9–15, 1970, and the final meeting at the same venue August 25–September 3, 1981. ARCIC I published *The Final Report* in 1982.

ARCIC II. On May 29, 1982, the eve of the feast of Pentecost, Pope John Paul II and Archbishop Robert Runcie, then archbishop of Canterbury, agreed to establish a new commission. ARCIC II's first three reports have been *Salvation and the Church* (1987), *Church as Communion* (1991), and *Life in Christ* (1994).

ARC-USA. The Anglican–Roman Catholic dialogue in the United States. The international term "Anglican" is used rather than the local term "Episcopalian."

BEM (Baptism, Eucharist and Ministry). See Lima Document.

Charism. The term derives from the Greek *charisma,* meaning gratuitous gift. Vatican II's Dogmatic Constitution On the Church asserts that, "There is only one Spirit who, according to his own richness and the need of the ministries, gives his different gifts for the welfare of the church (cf. 1 Cor 12:11)." Charisms belong to the nature of the church but are God's specific gifts to the faithful. A charism has been defined as "the

153

call of God, addressed to an individual, to a particular ministry in the community, which brings with it the ability to fulfill that ministry."

Collegiality. As used by the Roman Catholic Church, collegiality refers to the world-wide solidarity of bishops in communion (*koinonia*) with each other and the pope. This is especially evident in ecumenical councils of the church. ARCIC I, *The Final Report,* "Authority in the Church I," comments: "A primate exercises his ministry not in isolation but in collegial association with his brother bishops."

Conciliarity. Conciliar theory deals with the relationship between the pope and general councils of the church in proclaiming the church's faith on decisive matters of faith and morals. In the later Middle Ages, discontent with the papacy led to *conciliar* theories that full authority in the Catholic Church resides in a general council of all the bishops, summoned by the pope, but without his opinions of themselves carrying decisive weight. ARCIC I, *The Final Report,* "Authority in the Church I," declares that "[papal] primacy and conciliarity are complementary elements of *episcopé,*" while confessing that "it has often happened that one has been emphasized at the expense of the other, even to the point of serious imbalance."

Eschatology. This is the doctrine of the end or last things—in Greek: *eschaton*; e.g., "The last (*eschatos*) enemy to be destroyed is death" (1 Cor 15:26). Thus eschatology deals with things eternal. Eschatology interprets the apocalyptic (end-time or judgment) language and imagery of Scripture in which, for example, the Son of Man will return on the clouds of heaven, stars fall from heaven, fire will consume the earth, or our destiny will be written in heavenly books.

Full Communion. By their baptism into Christ, Christians are in communion with one another. This communion, though real, is imperfect through the division of the churches. The goal of ecumenism is the restoration of the churches to "full communion," expressed in the mutual recognition and acceptance of one another's sacraments and doctrine as authentic expressions of the catholic faith.

General Synod. The General Synod of the Church of England is its governing body. The archbishops of Canterbury and York are its joint presidents. The convocations of Canterbury and York combine to form a House of Bishops and a House of Clergy; to these are added a third house, the House of Laity. The General Synod must meet at least twice a year. Matters concerning doctrinal formulation, the services of the church, and the administration of the sacraments can be approved only in terms proposed by the House of Bishops.

Indefectibility. This is the belief that, despite human error and weakness, the church will never cease to be the church, witnessing to the truth. ARCIC I, *The Final Report,* "Authority in the Church II," states: "The Church is confident that the Holy Spirit will effectually enable it to fulfill its mission so that it will neither lose its essential character nor fail to reach its goal." A footnote adds: "This is the meaning of *indefectibility,* a term which does not speak of the church's lack of defects but confesses that, despite all its many weaknesses and failures, Christ is faithful to his promise that the gates of hell shall not prevail against it."

Infallibility. This denotes the preservation from error of the church, a general council, or a pope. In recent years most discussion has focused on papal infallibility. The pope is "protected from error" on those (rare) occasions when he speaks *ex cathedra*; that is, when he is formally defining for the whole church, doctrine concerning faith or morals.

Koinonia. This is a Greek term translated variously "fellowship" or "communion." Perhaps its best known use is at the close of 2 Corinthians: "The grace of the Lord Jesus Christ and the love of God and the fellowship (*koinonia*) of the Holy Spirit be with you all." The Anglican–Roman Catholic International Commission took *koinonia* in its sense of communion as a fundamental concept in interpreting the nature of the church, explaining in the introduction of *The Final Report* that "Although *koinonia* is never equated with 'church' in the New Testament, it is the term that most aptly expresses the mystery underlying the various images of the Church."

Lima Document. In Lima, Peru, in 1982, the Faith and Order Commission of the World Council of Churches presented the text, *Baptism, Eucharist and Ministry* often referred to as BEM. The *Lima Document* indicated a growing convergence among mainline churches in the doctrinal areas of baptism, Eucharist, and ministry.

Lima Liturgy. The *Lima Liturgy* has been drawn up to celebrate the remarkable convergence expressed in the *Lima Document.*

Magisterium. In Roman Catholic usage this is the teaching authority of the church. In modern times it has come to mean almost exclusively the teaching function of the bishops. This is often termed "Ordinary *Magisterium.*" When this teaching office is exercised in a "solemn" or "extraordinary" manner, it is termed "Extraordinary *Magisterium.*" Such occasions are when an ecumenical council defines a doctrine or when a pope declares that he is speaking *ex cathedra,* that is, when he is formally defining for the whole church, doctrine concerning faith or morals.

NCCB (National Conference of Catholic Bishops). This is the conference of all the bishops of the Roman Catholic Church, residential, auxiliary, and retired, in the United States.

Pontifical Council for Promoting Christian Unity. This council, originally named the Secretariat for Promoting Christian Unity, was set up in 1960 in preparation for Vatican Council II. It was thought that the unity secretariat would deal chiefly with Protestant churches, but its responsibilities grew, beginning with its being given, on October 19, 1962, a status equivalent to that of the other conciliar commissions.

Praxis. Praxis is a deliberate implementation of that which actually influences the way we live and work consistent with our faith. It is a practical, conscious consequence of our acceptance of the Christian Gospel.

Primacy. The Roman Catholic church affirms that the bishop of Rome, or pope, is bishop of the first—or primary see—of the church and is the head of the episcopal college. The Latin term is *prima sedes.*

Primate. Historically this is the title of the bishop of the first or primary see of a province—i.e., a group of neighboring dioceses, which form a unit. The archbishop of Canterbury is "Primate of all England" and the archbishop of York is "Primate of England."

Province. This is a group of neighboring dioceses, which form an ecclesiastical unit.

Congregation for the Doctrine of the Faith (CDF). This is the Vatican office of the Roman Catholic Church charged with theological oversight of church doctrine.

Subsidiarity. The principle as stated by Pope Pius XI in *Quadragesimo Anno* (1931) is that "One should not withdraw from individuals and commit to the community what they can accomplish by their own enterprise and industry. So too it is an injustice and at the same time a grave evil and a disturbance of right order to transfer to a greater and higher association functions which can be performed and provided for by lesser and subordinate bodies."

Suffragan Bishop. In the Episcopal Church, a suffragan bishop acts as an assistant bishop in a given diocese, but is duly elected by the diocese. An assistant bishop, by contrast, can be appointed by the diocesan bishop.

Synod. In the Church of England the General Synod is the church's final decision making body. It is composed of three houses: bishops, clergy, and laity, thereby ensuring the full participation of elected laity in the church's decision making. Matters of doctrinal formulation, liturgy, and sacramental theology, however, have to be approved in terms proposed by the House of Bishops.

Tradition. Tradition, which is grounded in the original deposit of Christian faith given by God to the apostles, is the continuous stream of explanation and elucidation of that faith. Thus tradition is more than a body of doctrine, though the creeds are a prime example of the role of tradition in expressing the faith of the church in its early centuries. The church's tradition is revealed by the interaction of a complex of interrelated components, including Scripture, the creeds, the teachings of the councils of the church, the teaching role of the bishops, sacraments and liturgy, and the reception of doctrine by the whole church.

Uniate. A term used in referring to the Eastern Catholic Church. The oriental rites of the Catholic Church were said to retain their own languages, rites, and canon law while being in union (hence the term *uniate*) with the Roman Catholic Church. The Eastern Catholic Church is Catholic through their bishops' membership in the college of bishops presided over by the bishop of Rome. But they are also Eastern in that they have received the faith through the *handing on*, (*traditio*), of the East not the West.

Guide to Further Reading

Called to Full Unity: Documents on Anglican–Roman Catholic Relations, 1966–1983 (Washington: United States Catholic Conference, 1985).

Congar, Yves, *Diversity and Communion* (London: SCM Press, 1984. Also published by Twenty-Third Publications, Mystic, Conn.).

Ellis, Christopher J., *Together on the Way: A Theology of Ecumenism* (The British Council of Churches, Inter-Church House, 35–41 Lower Marsh, London SE1 7RL).

Pawley, Bernard and Margaret, *Rome and Canterbury Through Four Centuries* (London and Oxford: Mowbrays, 1974).

Runcie, Robert, *The Unity We Seek* (London: Darton Longman and Todd, 1989).

Rusch, William, *Reception: An Ecumenical Opportunity* (Philadelphia: Fortress Press, 1988).

LAITY

Anderson, James D. and Ezra Earl Jones, *Ministry of the Laity* (San Francisco: Harper and Row, 1986).

Audibert, A. *La laïcité* (Paris: Presses universitaires de la France, 1960).

Bradshaw, Paul F., "Lay-People in the Church: Some Models of Ministry," *Doctrine and Life 37* (1987) 386–399.

Bradshaw, Paul F., "Lay Ministry: Theories," *Doctrine and Life 37* (1987) 499–511.

Bradshaw, Paul F., "Patterns of Ministry: The Role of Laity in Liturgy," *Studia Liturgica 15* (1982/83) 49–64.

Bucy, Ralph D., ed. *The New Laity Between Church and World* (Waco, Texas: Word Books, 1978).

Campbell, Thomas Charles, and Yoshio Fukuyama, *The Fragmented Layman: An Empirical Study of Lay Attitudes* (Philadelphia: Pilgrim Press, 1970).

Concilium: Spirituality in the Church and World (New York: Paulist Press, 1965).

Congar, Yves, *Lay People in the Church: A Study for a Theology of the Laity,* translated by Donald Attwater (Westminster, Md.: Newman Press, 1957).

Coughlan, Peter, *The Hour of the Laity: Their Expanding Role* (Wilton, Conn.: Morehouse, 1991).

Cross, Claire, *Church and People, 1450–1660: The Triumph of the Laity in the English Church* (London: Fontana-Atlantic Highlands; New Jersey: Humanities Press, 1976).

Decree on the Apostolate of the Laity (*Apostolicam actuositatem,* November 18, 1965), in Austin P. Flannery, ed., *Documents of Vatican II* (Grand Rapids: William B. Eerdmans Publishing, 1975, 1984) 766–798.

Dome, Arnold B., *Agents of Reconciliation* (Philadelphia: Westminster, 1960).

Dozier, Verna, *The Authority of the Laity* (Washington: Alban Institute, 1982).

Foley, Gerald, *Empowering the Laity* (Kansas City: Sheed and Ward, 1986).

Gibbs, Mark, and Ralph Morton, *God's Frozen People: A Book for and about Christian Laymen* (Philadelphia: Westminster, 1965).

Guilmot, Paul, *Fin d'une Église cléricale? Le debat en France de 1945 a nos jours* (Paris: Cerf, 1969).

Kraemer, Hendrick, *A Theology of the Laity* (London: Westminster Press, 1958).

Manette, Maurice L., *Kindred Spirits: The Bonding of Religious and Laity* (Kansas City: Sheed and Ward, 1987).

Macquarrie, John, *The Faith of the People of God: A Lay Theology* (New York: Scribners, 1972).

Newman, John Henry, *On Consulting the Faithful in Matters of Doctrine* (New York: Sheed and Ward, 1961).

Oxford, Bishop of [Richard Harries], chair, *All are Called: Towards a Theology of the Laity.* Essays from a Working Party of the General Synod Board of Education (London: CIO Publishing, 1985).

Pastoral Constitution on the Church in the Modern World (*Gaudium et Spes,* December 7, 1965), in Austin P. Flannery, ed., *Documents of Vatican II* (Grand Rapids: William B. Eerdmans Publishing, 1975, 1984) 903–1014.

Rahner, Karl, *Theology for Renewal: Bishops, Priests, Laity,* translated by Cecile Hastings and Richard Strachan (New York: Sheed and Ward, 1964).

Roche, Douglas J., and Remi DeRoo, *Man to Man: A Frank Talk Between a Layman and a Bishop* (Milwaukee: Bruce, 1969).

Swidler, Leonard J., *Bishops and People* (Philadelphia: Westminster, 1970).

Sykes, Stephen, ed., *Authority in the Anglican Communion* (Toronto: Anglican Book Centre, 1987).

Thompsett, Fredrica Harris, "The Laity," in Stephen Sykes and John Booty, eds., *The Study of Anglicanism* (London-Philadelphia: SPCK/Fortress, 1988).

Thompsett, Fredrica Harris, *We Are Theologians. Strengthening the People of the Episcopal Church* (Cambridge: Cowley, 1989).

Thorman, Donald J., *The Emerging Layman: The Role of the Catholic Layman in America* (Garden City: Image Books, 1965).

Trueblood, Elton, *Your Other Vocation* (New York: Harper, 1962).

ANGLICAN-ROMAN CATHOLIC FAMILIES

Anglican-Roman Catholic Dialogue. "When Episcopalians and Roman Catholics Marry" (Los Angeles: 4112 North Washington Blvd., Los Angeles 90018, 1980).

Anglican-Roman Catholic International Commission. "Theology of Marriage and its Application to Mixed Marriages." Secretariat for Promoting Christian Unity, Information Service 32 (1976) 12–27.

Ecumenical Trends 14/6 (Graymoor: June 1985) deals with mixed marriages.

EDEO/NADEO Joint Standing Committee, *ARC Marriages: A Study of U.S. Couples Living Episcopal-Roman Catholic Marriages* (Los Angeles: St. Paul's Parish, May 5, 1981).

EDEO/NADEO Joint Standing Committee, "Pastoral Care for ARC Couples" (Los Angeles: 4112 Washington Blvd., 90018, 1982).

Falardeau, Ernest R., S.S.S., ed., *ARC Soundings: A U.S. Response to ARCIC I* (New York: University Press of America, 1990). A compilation of EDEO/NADEO studies from 1983–1985.

Illinois Episcopalian-Roman Catholic Bishops, *A Unique Grace:* A Statement on the Marriage Between Episcopal and Roman Catholic Christians in Illinois (Chicago: Catholic Conference of Illinois, 1991).

Kilcourse, George, *Ecumenical Marriage: An Orientation Booklet for Engaged Couples, Families, Pastoral Ministers, Religious Educators* (National Association of Diocesan Ecumenical Officers, 1987). An excellent, practical study which accomplishes its purpose to direct ecumenical couples and others to the horizons of the Church's ecumenical life. Discussion questions and a selected bibliography are included. Copies available: Office of Ecumenical Affairs, P.O. Box 942, Louisville, KY 40201.

"Louisiana Guidelines for Episcopal/RC Marriages," *Ecumenical Trends* 10 (Graymoor, 1981) 123-125.

J. Lynch, "Ecumenical Marriages" (Washington: Proceedings of the 35th Annual Convention, Canon Law Society of America, 1973) 33-54.

Johannes Cardinal Willebrands, "Mixed Marriages and Eucharistic Communion," *Catholic Mind* 79 (n.d.) 45-49.

ANGLICAN-ROMAN CATHOLIC COVENANTS

"Church of the Holy Apostles. The Anglican/Roman Catholic Congregation of Tidewater Sacramental Policies." *Ecumenical Trends* 9/1 (1980).

Hagen, Kenneth, et. al., *The Bible in the Churches: How Different Christians Interpret the Scriptures* (New York: Paulist Press, 1985).

Horgan, Thaddeus, S.A., *Inter-Parish Covenants* (Graymoor, n.d.).

"Knowing Christ Together: Implementing the Episcopal/Roman Catholic Covenant" (Chicago: Episcopal/Roman Catholic Covenant Commission, 1991).

Marx, Michael, O.S.B., *Protestants and Catholics on the Spiritual Life* (Collegeville: The Liturgical Press, 1965).

Parish Outreach Committee of the Ecumenical and Interfaith Commission of the Milwaukee Archdiocese, *That All May Be One: A Handbook for Parishes* (Milwaukee: 1984). Order from the Archdiocese, P.O. Box 2018, Milwaukee, WI 53201.

HUNTHAUSEN

Fransen, Piet, S.J., "Episcopal Conferences: Crucial Problem of the Council," *Ecumenism and Vatican II.* Ed., Charles O'Neill, S.J. (Milwaukee: The Bruce Publishing Co., 1964) 98-126.

Fransen, Piet, S.J., "Criticism of Some Basic Theological Notions in Matters of Church Authority," *Authority in the Church,* Piet Fransen, ed. *Annual Nuntia Lovaniensia* 26 (1983) 48-74.

Kloppenburg, Bonaventure, *The Ecclesiology of Vatican II,* tr. by Matthew J. O'Connell (Chicago: Franciscan Herald Press, 1974).

O'Leary, Paul, O.P., "Authority to Proclaim the Word of God, and the Consent of the Church," *Freiburger Zeitschrift für Philosophie und Theologie* 29 (1982) 239–251.

Rahner, Karl, "On the Relationship Between the Pope and the College of Bishops," *Theological Investigations* 10 (London: Darton, Longman and Todd, 1973).

Sullivan, Francis A., *Magisterium: Teaching Authority in the Church* (New York: Paulist Press, 1983).

Tavard, George, "Is the Papacy an Object of Faith?" *One in Christ* 13 (1977) 220–228.

Tillard, Jean, *The Bishop of Rome,* tr. by John de Stage (London: SPCK, 1983).

Yarnold, Edward, J., S.J., "Primacy and Conciliarity," *Month* 238 (1977) 78–81.

JENKINS

Harrison, Ted, *The Durham Phenomenon* (London: Darton, Longman and Todd, 1985). This is very much a journalist's account of the issues. It contains a transcript of the television program, *Credo,* during which Jenkins made his remarks on the Virgin Birth and Resurrection.

Jenkins, David, *God Miracle and the Church of England* (London: SCM Press, 1987). Chapter 1, "The Nature of Christian Belief," is a speech by Jenkins to the General Synod of York on Sunday, July 6, 1986. The speech was a response to the House of Bishops' Report, *The Nature of Christian Belief.*

Jenkins, David and Rebecca, *Free To Believe* (London: BBC Books, 1991). Rebecca Jenkins authored the book but the preface claims that "The Outline . . . the arguments of each chapter and the draft of every page has been discussed again and again between the two authors" so that "the resulting book presents and represents David Jenkins' thoughts."

The Nature of Christian Belief: A Statement and Exposition by the House of Bishops of the General Synod of the Church of England (London: Church House Publishing, 1986). Although this report makes no mention of Bishop Jenkins, its immediate origin was a debate in General Synod on February 13, 1985. This debate itself originated from Jenkins' remarks on *Credo.*

CURRAN

Apostolic Constitution *Sapientia Christiana* on ecclesiastical universities and faculties in *Acta Apostolicae Sedis,* vol. 71, no. 7 (May 15, 1979).

Byron, William J., "Credentialed, Commissioned and Free," *America* (August 23, 1986) 69–71.

Congregation for the Doctrine of the Faith, "Instruction on the Ecclesial Vocation of the Theologian," *Origins* 20:9 (July 1, 1990).

Conklin, Richard, "The Vatican Challenges Catholic Academia's Declaration of Independence," *Notre Dame Magazine* (Summer 1986) 43–44.

Fogarty, Gerald P., "Dissent at Catholic University: The Case of Henry Poels," *America* (October 11, 1986) 180–184.

Franklin, R. W., "Lessons from the Past Illuminate Curran Affair," *College Teaching* 35:2 (Spring 1987) 50.

McCormick, Richard A., "L'Affair Curran," *America* (April 5, 1986) 261–267.

McCormick, Richard A., "The Search for Truth in the Catholic Context," *America* (November 8, 1986) 276–281.

McMillan, Liz, "Liberal Theologian May Sue Catholic U. over Suspension," *The Chronicle of Higher Education* (January 21, 1987) 13.

Mojzes, Paul, "Ecumenism under Vatican Threat," *Journal of Ecumenical Studies* 23:2 (Spring 1987) 358–359.

Wright, J. Robert, "Open Letter to the Members of ARCIC II," *Journal of Ecumenical Studies* 23:2 (Spring 1987) 354.

ORDINATION OF WOMEN

Canada's Anglican–Roman Catholic Dialogue, "Reflections on the Experience of Women's Ministries," *Origins* 21:38 (1992).

The Committee for the Full Participation of Women in the Church, *Reaching for Wholeness: The Participation of Women in the Episcopal Church* (Episcopal Church Foundation, 1987). This report was prepared for distribution to the 69th General Convention for the Episcopal Church, Detroit, Michigan, July 1988.

Congregation for the Doctrine of the Faith. *Declaration on the Question of the Admission of Women to the Ministerial Priesthood, with Commentary* (Washington: United States Catholic Conference, 1977).

Darling, Pamela W., *New Wine* (Boston: Cowley Publications, 1994).

Donovan, Mary S., *Women Priests in the Episcopal Church* (Cincinnati: Forward Movement Press, 1988). This book opens with a most helpful history of the events which led to the ordination of women to the priesthood in the Episcopal Church (3–28). It then tells the story of a number of women priests. It ends with a reflection on the effects of the ordination of women as priests (173–180).

Episcopal Ministry. The report of the Archbishops' Group on the Episcopate 1990 (London: Church House Publishing, 1990).

Faculty of Catholic Theological Union at Chicago. *Women and the Priesthood: Future Directions, A Call to Dialogue* (Collegeville: The Liturgical Press, 1978). Responses to the Vatican Declaration.

Gardiner, Anne Marie, S.S.N.D., ed., "Women and Catholic Priesthood: An Expanded Vision" (New York: Paulist Press, 1976). Proceedings of the Detroit Ordination Conference, Essays from Catholic Theologians.

Harrison, Ted, *Much Beloved Daughter* (Wilton, Conn.: Morehouse-Barlow, 1985). This is a biography of Florence Tim Oi Li.

Lambeth Convention 1988, *The Truth Shall Make You Free* (London: Church House, 1988) 115–16.

Report of the Archbishop of Canterbury's Commission on Communion and Women in the Episcopate 1989, Robert Eames, Chairman (London: Church House, 1989). This is usually referred to as the *Eames Report.*

Spiazzi, Raimondo, et. al., *The Order of Priesthood: Nine Commentaries on the Vatican Decree Interinsigniores* (Huntington: *Our Sunday Visitor,* 1978). Essays provide positive positions on the declaration.

Sumner, David E., *The Episcopal Church's History 1945–1985* (Wilton, Conn.: Morehouse-Barlow, 1987). Chapters 2 and 3 (7–30) are titled "Women become General Convention Deputies" and "The Path to Women's Ordination."

Swidler, Leonard and Arlene, *Women Priests: A Catholic Commentary on the Vatican Declaration* (New York: Paulist Press, 1977).

Tavard, George, *Women in Christianity* (Notre Dame: University of Notre Dame Press, 1973). Excellent survey and analysis.

Van der Meer, Haye, S.J. *Women Priests in the Catholic Church* (Philadelphia: Temple University Press, 1973). (Original in Dutch in 1963.) An early work with detailed documentation which calls for an open re-examination of the issue.

Women Priests: Obstacle to Unity? This publication of the Catholic Truth Society in London (DO576) contains the official Roman Catholic *Declaration* and *Commentary* from the Congregation for the Doctrine of the Faith. It also has correspondence on this subject between Archbishops Coggan and Runcie and Pope Paul VI; also correspondence between Cardinal Willebrands and Archbishop Runcie.

THE PASTORAL PROVISION

Fichter, Joseph H., "Blaming Women Priests: A Note on the Anglican Split," *Church* (Winter 1987).

Fichter, Joseph H., "Churches in Conflict: Comparative Problems of Episcopalians and Roman Catholics in America," *The Christian Challenge* (June 1988).

Fichter, Joseph H., "Lost Opportunities: Catholics and the Anglican Rite," *Canadian Catholic Review* (February 1989).

Fichter, Joseph H., "Married Priests and Ecumenism," *The Ecumenist* (January–February 1988).

Fichter, Joseph H., "The Ordination of Episcopal Priests," *America* (September 17–24, 1988).

Fichter, Joseph H., "Parishes for Anglican-Usage," *America* (November 14, 1987) and *Catholic Digest* (May 1988).

Fichter, Joseph H., *The Pastoral Provisions—Married Catholic Priests* (Kansas City: Sheed and Ward, 1989).

Fichter, Joseph H., "Rome Welcomes Married Priests," *Commonweal* (March 24, 1988).

Tegels, Aelred, O.S.B., "Anglican Use Liturgy," *Worship* 59 (May 1985).

Authors

The Third Standing Committee of the Episcopal Diocesan Ecumenical Officers and the National Diocesan Ecumenical Officers (EDEO/NADEO) is made up of:

The Reverend David Bird, Ph.D. (EDEO Co-chair)
Rector, Grace Church, Georgetown, Washington, D.C.

Sr. Joan McGuire, O.P., S.T.D. (NADEO Co-chair)
Governing Board Member, Dominican Sisters
St. Catharine, Kentucky

E. Rozanne Elder, Ph.D. (EDEO)
Director, Institute of Cistercian Studies
Western Michigan University, Kalamazoo

R. William Franklin, Ph.D. (EDEO)
Michael Blecker Professor of the Humanities
St. John's University, Collegeville
Beginning 1993 SPRL Professor of History and World Mission and Professor of Anglican Studies
The General Theological Seminary, New York

The Reverend Dennis Mikulanis, S.T.D. (NADEO)
Director, Ecumenical and Interreligious Affairs, Diocese of San Diego

The Reverend Emmanuel Sullivan, S.A., Ph.D. (NADEO)
Ecumenical Officer for Diocese of Arundel and Brighton, England